OHIO BREWERIES

OHIO
BREWERIES

RICK ARMON

STACKPOLE
BOOKS

Published by
STACKPOLE BOOKS
5067 Ritter Road
Mechanicsburg, PA 17055
www.stackpolebooks.com

The author and publisher encourage readers to visit the breweries and sample
their beers and recommend that those who consume alcoholic beverages travel with a nondrinking driver.

Printed in the United States of America

10 9 8 7 6 5 4 3 2 1

FIRST EDITION

Cover design by Tessa J. Sweigert

Labels and logos are used with the permission of the breweries

Library of Congress Cataloging-in-Publication Data

Armon, Rick.
    Ohio breweries / Rick Armon. — 1st ed.
        p.   cm.
    Includes index.
    ISBN-13: 978-0-8117-0868-5 (pbk.)
    ISBN-10: 0-8117-0868-3 (pbk.)
    1. Bars (Drinking establishments)—Ohio—Guidebooks.   2. Breweries—
Ohio—Guidebooks.   I. Title.
TX950.57.O3A76   2011
647.95771—dc23
                                                    2011017021

To Wendy—
Thanks for being such a great,
understanding wife

Contents

Acknowledgments

It was May 4, 2010—election night in Ohio—and I was sitting at my desk at the *Akron Beacon Journal* bored. Unlike what voters or the general public might think, election night is pretty darned boring. You sit for hours waiting for election results to come. Then they do and you quickly call candidates to get their reactions and write furiously to meet an unrealistic deadline. So for about a half hour, you're obnoxiously busy.

So there I was waiting for results. Bored. I don't even know why, but I shot off an e-mail to Lew Bryson, a well-respected beer blogger, magazine writer, and author of *New York Breweries* and *Pennsylvania Breweries* and co-author of *New Jersey Breweries*. Lew and I had met years earlier when he completed the New York book and I was co-writing a beer column at the *Democrat and Chronicle* newspaper in Rochester, New York. He was a likable guy—someone who enjoyed beer but wasn't a beer snob. Through the years, I had kept in touch and occasionally used him as a source for newspaper stories about beer.

When I had moved to Ohio in 2005, Lew had encouraged me to write the Ohio version of his other books. I had thought about it and always decided against it. For some reason, that night I asked Lew if Stackpole Books had ever found someone to write the Ohio book. The publisher hadn't. Lew put in a good word for me. And now here's the book.

So I must thank Lew. And also curse him. He really didn't warn me about how difficult the task of writing about fifty breweries would be. During my trips across the state, we exchanged e-mails, with me asking him if he had encountered similar obstacles. He had. And I'll get into some of those later in the book because anyone who decides to visit all these breweries will likely run into the same hurdles.

The Ohio breweries also deserve a warm and hearty thank you, especially Anheuser-Busch InBev, MillerCoors, and Boston Beer Company. I had been warned that those larger companies would be unwilling to open their doors and talk about their operations. The exact opposite was true. They are passionate about their craft, proud of their connection with Ohio, and more than willing to share their stories.

I am really appreciative of all the help from John Najeway, one of the owners of Thirsty Dog Brewing Company in Akron. John and I have known each other for years, and he provided much encouragement and help along the way.

The *Akron Beacon Journal* also helped, allowing me to adjust my schedule. I worked Saturday through Wednesday at the newspaper, and drove around the state researching and writing on Thursdays and Fridays. For nearly four months, I worked seven days a week.

That's why my wife Wendy deserves kudos as well. She put up with months of me being away on overnight trips and holing up in a converted office at our house to write and re-write. While I focused on the book, she had to babysit our crazy dog, a lab-whippet mix that thrives on attention.

Lastly, I wanted to extend a special thanks to my mom, Jean Armon. She died from cancer while I was researching and writing this book. We talked often by phone while I was crisscrossing the state. She was a nurse and worried that I was drinking too much. I wish she could have seen the book published.

Introduction

Welcome to Ohio. This book isn't about history and breweries that died out long ago. It's about the here and now—a guidebook to the state's current brewing industry.

It's about industry giants that call Ohio home, such as Anheuser-Busch InBev in Columbus and MillerCoors in Trenton. It's about the well-respected and big craft brewers such as Boston Beer Company in Cincinnati and Great Lakes Brewing Company in Cleveland. And it's about the tiny operations such as Quarter Barrel Brewery & Pub in Oxford and Great Black Swamp Brewing in Toledo.

This is also a travel book, providing insight into Ohio-made beer and giving you a reason to sample the state's offerings.

First, let's start with a little background about Ohio. It's the seventh most populous state in the nation with 11.5 million people. Unlike many other states, Ohio has plenty of major cities scattered throughout: Akron, Cincinnati, Cleveland, Columbus, Dayton, and Toledo, most of them with a history steeped in manufacturing.

Although it is home to award-winning breweries, Ohio has long been overshadowed by other states when it comes to beer-making. Perhaps the reason involves sheer numbers. Ohio has forty-nine breweries, not counting small operations at private clubs. Just to the north, Michigan has more than sixty craft breweries. Just to the east, Pennsylvania has more than seventy operations. Colorado has more than ninety.

Ohio has been slower to embrace the craft brewery revolution. Why? Brewers blame it partly on the high taxes and permit fees here. The numbers are changing, though. Thanks in part to the rise of nanobreweries—tiny operations brewing on small systems that even some skilled homebrewers use—Ohio has seen a spike in new breweries. In 2010 and 2011 alone, at least eleven opened.

My job was to visit them all. Over the course of four short months, I put nearly 7,000 miles on my black Toyota Rav4 while crisscrossing the state over and over to visit breweries. I sampled more than 400 different beers. At the end, my pants were tight. Too tight. My regular exercise regime took a backseat to beer sampling. My one regret is that I didn't weigh myself at the beginning of this adventure.

BREWERY LOCATIONS

book page

BREWERY LOCATIONS   *book page*

How to Use This Book

The brewing industry is a volatile one. For example, 110 breweries opened nationwide while another 52 closed in 2009. Ohio is no exception. Eight breweries opened for business in 2010, while another five closed their doors.

What's this mean? This book includes short chapters on every brewery—except for private operations at private clubs—that had a beer manufacturing permit from the state by the end of 2010. Some of those breweries had yet to open. By the time you read this, the brewery landscape in Ohio could easily have changed with more breweries opening and closing. For example, Black Squirrel Brewing Company in Kent and Bottle House Brewing Company in Cleveland Heights were scheduled to open in mid-2011. Some other details, such as hours, may have changed, so be sure to call ahead or at least check out their websites.

At its heart, this is a beer travel book. It breaks down the state into different regions and showcases not only the breweries, but also other potential tourist attractions in those areas for beer drinkers. Some of the breweries featured here—in particular, Anheuser-Busch InBev, MillerCoors, and Boston Beer—aren't open for tours. It may seem odd to include them in a travel book about breweries, but they are part of the Ohio brewery industry and deserve to be featured.

This book isn't a rating guide of breweries or beers; there are plenty of websites devoted to ratings. I've also tried to avoid overwhelming you with industry jargon, although a glossary is provided at the end.

Many of the chapters are focused on the personalities behind the brewery. Let's face it, people often make the most interesting stories. So enjoy the ride.

Cheers!

Big Boys

Ohio is unusual—but not unique—in the beer industry when it comes to big national breweries. The Buckeye State is home to Anheuser-Busch InBev in Columbus and MillerCoors in Trenton.

These companies happen to make the best-selling and most popular beer brands in the country, if not the world: Budweiser, Miller, and Coors. Combined, these two Ohio giants can produce more than 20 million barrels of beer or 6.6 billion bottles a year. To put these numbers in perspective, the local brewpub on the corner would be thrilled to make more than 1,200 barrels annually.

Ohio is one of only six states with both Anheuser-Busch InBev and MillerCoors breweries. The others are California, Colorado, Georgia, Texas, and Virginia.

But Ohio has another national powerhouse, as well, albeit on a smaller level. The Boston Beer Company's Samuel Adams Brewery in Cincinnati has the capacity to make 600,000 to 700,000 barrels a year.

So what's this all mean? Well, Ohio should take a bow because it's one of the largest beer-producing states in the nation. How could it not be with these three major breweries here? Unfortunately, the Beer Institute, a trade and lobbying group in Washington, D.C., no longer ranks states by production. But it's safe to say that Ohio is in the top five.

Anheuser-Busch InBev and MillerCoors in particular take a lot of knocks from beer geeks and even smaller brewers who complain about the major brands being just fizzy yellow water made for the uneducated masses. But they dominate the U.S. beer industry, controlling about eighty percent of the market. In other words, people love their products.

More than one thousand Ohioans work at the Anheuser-Busch InBev and MillerCoors breweries. They put a lot of care into making beer. As any brewer will tell you, the hardest beer to make is a light American-style pilsner. Why? You can't hide any flaws in a lighter beer. And Anheuser-Busch InBev and MillerCoors are able to turn out lighter beers with the same quality and consistency day after day, despite the brands being made at plants around the country. It's amazing when you really think about it.

The Anheuser-Busch InBev, MillerCoors, and Samuel Adams breweries in Ohio are marvels, both in terms of sheer size and the technology involved in the beer-making. It's funny to see brewers sit in front of computer monitors as they track every step of the brewing process or to watch robots load delivery trucks in enormous warehouses. It's fascinating to see quality-control labs filled with people running scientific experiments on the beer to make sure that it's perfect for the consumer. And it's awe-inspiring to see gigantic brewhouses and fermenters.

The only disappointing aspect of my Ohio visits is that the major breweries aren't open for public tours. It's a shame. If you're dying for a look inside one of these major breweries, however, you're in luck if you're willing to travel. Anheuser-Busch InBev provides tours at its plants in St. Louis, Missouri; Fairfield, California; Fort Collins, Colorado; Jacksonville, Florida; and Merrimack, New Hampshire. MillerCoors provides tours at its breweries in Milwaukee, Wisconsin, and Golden, Colorado. Samuel Adams offers tours at its Boston brewery.

Anheuser-Busch InBev

700 Schrock Road, Columbus, OH 43229
614-888-6644 • www.anheuser-busch.com

Kevin Lee has a cool job. And everyone knows it. Whether he's sitting with the governor or at a party with a group of surgeons, people always want to talk with him as opposed to anybody else in the room.

That's because as general manager of Anheuser-Busch InBev's Columbus plant, he oversees production of the world's most popular beers in one of the largest, most modern breweries in the United States. He fields questions all the time. What's it like working at the brewery? How much beer do you make? How's the InBev takeover going? Do you get to drink beer at work?

"You could think of whatever job might be the most exciting and you bring up that you head up the Columbus brewery and that's where all the conversation goes," Lee said with a laugh. "It's all about the beer. Now, I think if there were a professional athlete there I would probably be second . . . (former Ohio State University football coach) Jim Tressel and me? Jim Tressel is going to be the more popular guy."

Some of the mystique about the brewery certainly lies with the iconic Budweiser brand and the company's rich heritage. Anheuser-Busch is known almost as much for its television commercials and the famous Clydesdales as the beer itself. Ohioans are as curious as the rest of the nation because the Columbus brewery isn't open to the public for tours and people want to know what goes on there.

The brewery itself is highly visible, sitting on 221 acres and bounded by Interstates 71 and 270, north of downtown Columbus. Fifty percent of the property, which includes a picnic area and softball field, is still undeveloped. Tens of thousands of motorists pass by every day, catching a whiff of the brewery and a glimpse of the huge yellow towers with the words Budweiser and Bud Light on the side.

The plant—one of twelve Anheuser-Busch breweries in the country—opened in 1968 and at first could make 1.6 million barrels a year. The company has invested heavily in the site through the years, pumping $500 million into the plant since 1995 alone to modernize and expand. Today, employees work twenty-four hours a day, seven days a week, and produce 10.7 million barrels a year.

Half a million cases a day roll off the production line. The four bottling lines and three canning lines can produce about 1,200 bottles and 2,000 cans a minute. The plant doesn't make every Anheuser-Busch brand, but it produces the core ones—Budweiser, Bud Light, and Michelob.

"It's exciting to work for a company that makes what is considered the largest brand of the world and the flagship brand of the world," Lee said. "And we would consider that's the best brand in the world."

The Columbus plant received a special honor in 2011 when the company named the plant its best brewery in North America. The Columbus facility beat out seventeen other Anheuser-Busch InBev breweries; they were judged on various criteria, including quality, productivity, safety, work environment, and management. Ohioans love

Beers brewed: Year-round: Budweiser, Bud Light, Bud Ice, Bud Select, Select 55, Michelob, Michelob Light, Michelob Ultra, Michelob Amber Bock, Busch, Busch Light, Busch NA, Natural Light, Natural Ice, O'Doul's, and O'Doul's Amber.

The Pick: Try a Bud Light. It's been the best-selling beer in the United States since 2001, when it knocked the King of Beers, Budweiser, from the top spot. It's light and crisp and can't be beat on a hot day. It's the best-selling beer for a reason.

Anheuser-Busch. The company enjoyed a 57.9 percent market share in the state in 2010, much higher than the 48 percent nationwide average, Lee said.

The plant itself is a marvel in terms of sheer size, technology, and cleanliness. Unlike smaller production breweries where everything is housed under one roof, the Anheuser-Busch plant is spread out over a couple of buildings. One of the more impressive sights is the truck loading area. While it may not sound exciting, the company has automated the process. Instead of people driving forklifts around loading beer onto delivery trucks, the work is done by robots. They buzz slowly around, picking up and dropping off crates of beer.

Perhaps the most exciting part of the day comes at 3:30 P.M., when the tasting panel gets together to sample the beer and make sure it's up to snuff. They sample everything from the beer heading out to the store the next day to the water coming into the plant.

Anheuser-Busch prides itself on making sure the beer produced at its plant in St. Louis, for example, tastes the same as the beer produced in Columbus, Newark, and Los Angeles. That is a tremendous accomplishment, especially for making a lighter product that's more susceptible to off flavors.

"Brewing is an art and a science," Lee said. "The art aspect of it is because of the variation with incoming materials. Year-to-year grains and hops. The nature of the growing seasons and the changes. We do a lot of work upstream to decrease that variability of that taste."

Anheuser-Busch InBev

Opened: 1968.
Owner: Anheuser-Busch InBev.
Brewer: Jennifer Eckstein.
Production: 10.7 million barrels.
Distribution: Global, but this plant sends beer to forty-six states. The core area is Ohio, Michigan, and parts of Kentucky, Indiana, and West Virginia.
Hours: The brewery is not open to the public.
Tours: None at the Columbus plant. If you really want to visit an Anheuser-Busch brewery, tours are available at the plants in St. Louis, Missouri; Fairfield, California; Fort Collins, Colorado; Jacksonville, Florida; and Merrimack, New Hampshire.
Take-out beer: None.
Parking: None available.

MillerCoors

2525 Wayne Madison Road, Trenton, OH 45067
513-896-9200 • www.millercoors.com

Not many people outside of southwestern Ohio know that MillerCoors has a brewery in the state. It's easy to overlook. For starters, the brewery is in a rural area surrounded by cornfields and well off the beaten path of travelers. Even while driving by, there's no giant sign identifying the plant as a MillerCoors facility. It could be just another manufacturing site.

The nearest city is Trenton, a town of less than 9,000. And when people hear there's a MillerCoors plant in Trenton, many automatically think of Trenton, New Jersey. The geography issue has even tripped up job candidates who traveled to New Jersey and then called the brewery to say they're lost.

"Needless to say we didn't hire them," plant manager Jon Hussey said, laughing.

MillerCoors has tried to promote itself more as an Ohio company and raise its profile in recent years, including having local radio ads mention Trenton, Ohio, instead of Milwaukee, Wisconsin. The company also has done plenty of outreach in the community by sponsoring events to get its name out.

The Trenton brewery, built in 1981, is one of eight major plants in the MillerCoors network, producing such national favorites as Miller Lite, Miller Genuine Draft, and Coors Light. The company chose Ohio for a couple of reasons. The state is well-positioned in the Midwest, making it a great spot for distribution. Then there's the water.

"You need a lot of water to make beer, and the Ohio aquifer is one of the largest freshwater aquifers in the country," Hussey said. "We're on top of a very large supply of water."

An odd fact is that the brewery sat mothballed for ten years after it was built. At the time, Bud Light had snared away some market share from Miller Lite, and Miller didn't need so much pro-

Beers brewed: Miller High Life, Miller High Life Light, Milwaukee's Best, Milwaukee's Best Light, Milwaukee's Best Ice, Miller Genuine Draft, Genuine Draft 64, Icehouse, Lite, Lite Ice, Red Dog, Olde English, Mickey's, Steel Reserve, Coors Light, Keystone Light, and Keystone Ice.

The Pick: Miller Genuine Draft. I have fond memories of drinking MGD after college. A friend and I would go to a neighborhood bar, order chicken wings, play pinball, and drink a few MGDs. The beer is crisp and dry and a perfectly acceptable lawnmower beer.

duction. Miller—this was before the merger with Coors—also had gone through a major building boom and opened breweries in North Carolina, Georgia, and California before the Trenton plant was constructed.

Fortunately, Miller Genuine Draft became more popular and the company needed to ramp up its beer-making. The bad part of that is that the Trenton plant was about ten years behind in technology. When it finally opened in 1991, the brewery had late 1970s technology.

The company has since upgraded throughout. The Trenton brewery now produces the second largest amount of beer in the MillerCoors network and serves all or parts of nine states. The brewing capacity is 10.6 million barrels a year. The company, which also does contract brewing, declined to identify the exact amount produced there.

The brewery itself, which employs about 550 people, is massive, covering 1.4 million square feet. The facility includes one kegging, five bottling, and five canning lines. The plant produces an average of 11 million bottles and cans a day.

"It's awe-inspiring, quite frankly," said Dedra Flournoy, the human resources manager who previously worked in the automotive field. "The amount of the barrelage that we produce. The complexity of the operations here. It's a manufacturing experience like none other. Just the speed. It's astonishing and impressive."

MillerCoors leaders are especially pleased that the Trenton plant is the most efficient brewery in the company from a cost standpoint. Hussey attributes that to running a lean operation and a collaborative relationship between union and management.

"We've been told that it's one of the most cost-effective breweries in the world," he said. "That's a pretty big source of pride to know you're doing something as efficiently as some of the best organizations in the world."

But that's not the only thing Hussey and others are proud of. The company also is trying to be a good corporate citizen when it comes to the environment. In 2007, the plant was sending about twenty tons of waste a month—mostly cardboard, glass, plastic, and aluminum—to a landfill. By January 2010, the brewery had reduced that by ninety-five percent by instituting an aggressive recycling program. The remaining five percent is being shipped to an Indianapolis company to be burned for energy.

The recycling initiative was led by a regular worker. The brewery was founded on the concept of a team and that's taken seriously, Flournoy said.

Brewery leaders also are proud about reducing their water usage. The plant uses about 3 million gallons of water a day, down from 3.5 million. The company was able to accomplish that by making improvements to its wastewater treatment plant and encouraging workers to pay more attention to turning off the water.

"There's a strong work ethic in this area. But certainly within this brewery, people really do put their muscle and integrity and brain power behind the label," she said. "So when people are drinking our product, they should know it's the people who are the differentiator. And we work every day to give our best to that product."

As for working at the brewery, Hussey, Flournoy, and others said they love it. When asked what people say when they learn he works at the brewery, Hussey responded: "Man, are you lucky."

MillerCoors

Opened: 1991.

Owner: MillerCoors.

Brewer: Paul DeCou.

Production: 10.6 million-barrel capacity.

Distribution: Ohio, Indiana, Kentucky, Michigan, and parts of Pennsylvania, New York, Illinois, Tennessee, and West Virginia.

Hours: The brewery is not open to the public.

Tours: None at the Trenton brewery. If you would like to visit a MillerCoors plant, the company does provide tours at its breweries in Milwaukee, Wisconsin, and Golden, Colorado.

Take-out beer: None.

Parking: None available.

Boston Beer Company / Samuel Adams

SAMUEL ADAMS®

1625 Central Parkway, Cincinnati, OH 45214
513-412-3200 • www.samueladams.com

Jim Koch knew he had to make a major change at the Hudepohl-Schoenling brewery when Boston Beer Company bought the facility in 1997. The two brew kettles were stainless steel and that wouldn't do. Koch wanted copper kettles, which impart a certain sense of quality and brewing tradition in the beer industry.

"The kettles really make the most powerful statement of who we are," Koch said during a personal tour of the brewhouse. "The other kettles were perfectly functional. But they didn't embody who we are."

He even named them after his father and great-great-grandfather, who both worked in the beer industry. The small circular doors used to peer into the kettles are inscribed with their names: Charles and Louis. Charles Koch, in fact, had worked at the brewery now owned by his son, and Louis had devised the original recipe for Samuel Adams Boston Lager.

So who is Boston Beer? Well, here's a refresher if you've been living under a rock for the last twenty years. It's a brewery that helped launch the craft beer movement in the 1980s and was the fifth-largest brewer in the United States in 2009, according to the Brewers Association. Boston Beer, which makes the popular lineup of Samuel Adams beers, also is the country's largest craft brewer.

The history of Boston Beer, now a publicly traded company on the New York Stock Exchange, is well-documented. Koch discovered a recipe in his family's attic for Louis Koch Lager, the beer that would become Boston Lager. He decided to name the brand after Samuel Adams, the patriot and brewer from Revolutionary War times.

The beer made its debut in 1984 and Koch opened a brewery in Boston in 1988. As the Samuel Adams brand became more popular, the company brewed on contract at various facilities—and took criticism from major brewers about that—before

Beers brewed: Year-round: Samuel Adams Boston Lager and Sam Adams Light. Boston Beer also produces more than thirty seasonal, rotating, and special beers.

The Pick: It would be easy to select Samuel Adams Boston Lager, a beer that turned me on to craft beer and is still one of my all-time favorites. But give the seasonal Chocolate Bock a try. It's an ale made with cocoa and has a major chocolate and velvety finish that any chocolate lover will enjoy.

buying the Hudepohl-Schoenling plant. The company also operates a brewery in Breinigsville, Pennsylvania. Despite the brewery's growth, Koch is quick to point out that Samuel Adams still makes up less than one percent of all beer sales in the United States.

As for the Cincinnati story, Koch grew up in the community. It's a story that seems almost too good to be true: Native son moves away, becomes a huge success, and returns to revive the grand brewing tradition in his hometown. And that is all true. But Koch freely admits that Boston Beer is in Cincinnati for business reasons as well as sentimental ones.

Samuel Adams had been brewed on contract at the Hudepohl-Schoenling brewery. One day, the owners approached Koch about buying the facility, saying they might have to otherwise shutter the plant. Koch figured it was the perfect size for Boston Beer. The brewery still produces beer in craft brewer–sized batches, 170 barrels at a time, and can produce 600,000 to 700,000 barrels a year. The production brewery, which isn't open for public tours, is made up of several buildings and, with space for expansion, now covers a whole city block in the Over-the-Rhine neighborhood, an area that once housed all of Cincinnati's major brewers. Today, the neighborhood is a downtrodden area near downtown that's filled with three- and four-story row buildings that once had retail establishments on the street level and apartments above. The buildings, with Italianate and Greek Revival architecture, were likely gorgeous in their time, but many have fallen into disrepair and are vacant.

Koch, a charming man who's quick to share his opinion and stories about beer-making, never envisioned his brewery growing as large as it has.

"My original business plan, which is an embarrassment, was to get to 5,000 barrels," he said. "I thought it would take five years and then it would level off. In defense of that egregiously erroneous number, that was realistic in 1984. When you looked at the handful of microbreweries that were out there and looked at their volume and the market, it was a realistic number."

Koch, who often appears in advertising campaigns for the beer, remains intimately involved with every aspect of the brewing process. (He even insisted on personally providing my tour at the Cincinnati plant.) As an example of his attention to detail, he recalled the story of Samuel Adams Latitude 48, a dry-hopped India pale ale first released in 2010.

The beer had been brewed and was ready to be bottled at 8 A.M. But there was one hitch. Koch wanted to sample the final batch before giving the go-ahead. The company used a medical courier to ship a sample to his house. At 5:45 A.M., he was in his kitchen tasting away. It got the okay.

Nothing is shipped to the public without his final approval. He said he has no qualms about killing a beer in the process if he doesn't enjoy it. Such was the case with an experimental chocolate chili beer.

"Chili is a skin irritant," Koch said, laughing. "It's exactly the same compound that's in tear gas. It doesn't belong in your mouth. That would be my theory. I'm not saying I'm right or wrong but I'm saying I nixed it because I can. It's worked out so far because we've had a lot of successful beers and I trust my palate."

Boston Beer continues to experiment with different styles and ingredients. The company is known for putting together some avant-garde beers, including Infinium, a beer made with Germany's Weihenstephan brewery that resembles champagne and is sold in a wine bottle with a cork, and Utopias, a beer with twenty-seven percent alcohol that's sold in a kettle-shaped decanter.

"When I started, it was pretty easy to be innovative and now the boundaries are more out there even for us as we're creating new beers," Koch said. "As we do that, I'm trying to make sure they meet our quality standard, which is 'Is this beer a pleasure to drink?' and if it's not a pleasure to drink, even if it's extreme and innovative and radical, there's no point. Ultimately, the reason to drink beer is that it gives you pleasure."

Boston Beer Company / Samuel Adams

Opened: Boston Beer Company purchased the Hudepohl-Schoenling brewery in 1997.

Owner: Boston Beer Company.

Brewer: Jim Koch.

Production: 600,000 to 700,000 barrel capacity.

Distribution: The Cincinnati plant supplies the Midwest and South in the U.S. and some overseas countries.

Hours: The brewery is not open to the public.

Tours: None at the Cincinnati brewery. If you would like to see a Samuel Adams brewery in operation, the Boston brewery offers tours.

Take-out beer: None.

Parking: None available.

Ohio's Beer Economy

Beer is big business in Ohio. The Beer Institute and the National Beer Whole-salers Association, both lobbying groups based in Washington, D.C., have proven that. They estimated in their 2010 "Beer Serves America" report that the beer industry—from breweries to distributors to retailers—contributes $9 billion a year to the state economy.

Hard to believe? It's a lot easier when you start adding the numbers. There are nearly two thousand brewing jobs in Ohio. Those are just the people working at breweries, which range from little brewpubs to massive production facilities. About double that number work in the distribution field. Those are the people who get the beer from the breweries to the store shelves.

Then there are all the folks working at bars, restaurants, and stores who are selling or serving the beer. The Beer Institute and wholesalers group estimated that there were nearly forty-three thousand people directly relying on the industry in the state. By comparison, Wal-Mart—the state's biggest employer—has about fifty-four thousand workers in Ohio.

Ohio trails only California, Colorado, Texas, Missouri, Florida, and New York in terms of beer's economic impact on an individual state. California, with about three hundred breweries, topped the list at $33 billion.

The two groups also estimated the amount of tax generated by the beer industry in Ohio—a staggering $1.2 billion. That's the amount of business and personal taxes paid to the federal, state, and local governments each year. Another $416 million is paid in consumption taxes. Beer taxes for the consumer are relatively high in Ohio. The "Beer Serves America" report estimated that the government takes a 47 percent cut of any beer purchased.

The big reason that Ohio collects so much is that the state is a major beer producer. Ohio ranks as one of the largest beer-makers in the nation along with Colorado, California, and Texas in terms of sheer volume. It doesn't hurt that two of the world's largest brewers—

Anheuser-Busch InBev and MillerCoors—call Ohio home and make more than 20 million barrels a year between them.

The Boston Beer Company and Great Lakes Brewing, two of the largest craft brewers in the country, also make beer in the state. For years, Ohio had lagged behind many other states, such as Colorado and Michigan, when it came to craft breweries. But there has been a spate of openings in the state and Ohio is narrowing the gap.

Ohioans enjoy their beer, too. The per capita consumption is 23 gallons, slightly above the U.S. average of 21 gallons. For comparison, the per capita consumption of wine in Ohio is only 1.7 gallons. For some reason, Montana and New Hampshire lead the nation in terms of per capita beer consumption at 31.9 gallons. Utah is last with 12.4 gallons.

Cleveland and Cuyahoga County

Let's dispense with the Cleveland jokes. No humorous elbows about the "Mistake on the Lake" or the burning Cuyahoga River or anything like that. Those are, quite frankly, comments made most likely by someone who has never visited the city, a place filled with outstanding museums, orchestras, theaters, and restaurants. Oh, and downright friendly people. Sure, Cleveland has its issues, but what major city doesn't?

Cleveland is my hometown, a community of about 1.2 million people when you include all of Cuyahoga County and nearly 2.9 million when you include the eight-county metropolitan area. The city sits right where the Cuyahoga River dumps into Lake Erie. Cleveland was settled in the late 1790s and named after Gen. Moses Cleaveland, who helped survey the area. And yes, the city's name was spelled wrong and that's how it ended up Cleveland instead of Cleaveland.

The city grew into an industrial giant in the late nineteenth century thanks to steel and oil companies. As everyone knows, American steel mills and oil companies struggled and so did Cleveland. But the community has transformed itself and now has a much more diverse range of companies. Today, Cuyahoga County is home to such industry heavyweights as the Cleveland Clinic, IMG, Sherwin-Williams, American Greetings, Progressive, and Cliffs Natural Resources.

Cleveland is where I cut my beer teeth, albeit mostly on cheap, watery stuff in the late 1980s. I remain fiercely loyal to the community, even though the professional sports teams try my patience year after year.

Anyone interested in the craft brewing scene knows that Cleveland is where it's at in Ohio. And that's not a putdown of any other communities in the state. It just so happens that Cleveland is home to a slew of breweries—more than any other area in Ohio. It's also where the craft brewing revolution started in the state in 1988 thanks to a little—well, not so little anymore—brewpub known as Great Lakes Brewing Company.

Great Lakes has become one of the most respected and largest regional breweries in the country. Its success has inspired others to open breweries throughout the state.

Today, Cuyahoga County and Cleveland boast nine breweries. That's not counting a couple more that were slated to open after this book went to publication. And that's just within the county. There are many more just outside the county, but I put them in the chapter on Northeast Ohio since I needed to group the breweries by geography.

There are plenty of things to do in Cleveland besides drinking beer. That said, here's a rundown of a few great beer places.

- **The Winking Lizard Tavern** is a phenomenal spot to grab a beer. There are fourteen locations throughout Northeast Ohio and Columbus. The downtown Cleveland location (811 Huron Road, www.winkinglizard.com) is a hoot because it's in a triangular building and the rooms get smaller as you head toward the tip of the restaurant. The chain offers hundreds of draft and bottle selections ranging from the mundane Labatt to the high-end Oud Orval. The folks here really care about good beer, whether it's from around the world or your backyard. The restaurant also features the World Beer Tour, but more on that later.

- **The Harbor Inn** (1219 Main Avenue, 216-241-3232) is a special place for me. My wife and I had our first date there. It's best described as an old dive—and by old I mean established in 1895. The bar is in the Flats district, once Cleveland's party area along the Cuyahoga River. The bar had a tremendous beer selection back in the 1980s when most places were serving only major national brands and imports. The selection, which has since been overshadowed by other beer bars, is still good.

- **Warehouse District** (www.warehousedistrict.org). Cleveland's party district has moved from the Flats, but not far. It's migrated only a block or two to the Warehouse District downtown. It's an area filled with old warehouses converted into housing, offices, and specialty restaurants and bars, including the Cleveland ChopHouse & Brewery (see page 29).

- **Tremont** (www.restoretremont.com). Another Cleveland area worth visiting is Tremont, a neighborhood near downtown that used to be run-down but has seen a rebirth with numerous bars, restaurants, and artsy shops.

- **McNulty's Bier Markt** (1948 W. 25th Street, 216-274-1010, www.bier-markt.com) is the place to check out if you love Belgian beer. The bar, open 365 days a year, has been named by *Draft Magazine* as one of the best beer bars in North America. The Bier Markt features rotating drafts and eighty bottled beers, including many Belgian and Belgian-style brews. The bar is located just around the corner from Great Lakes Brewing Company. The operators of the Bier Markt have also opened their own brewery called Market Garden across the street.

Here are some other attractions in the area that you might want to make time to visit.

- **The West Side Market** (1979 W. 25th Street, www.westsidemarket .org), across the street from McNulty's, is the oldest public market in Cleveland. The giant indoor arcade is an absolute treasure that dates back to 1912. It features everything from fresh produce to bread to hard-to-find meats, such as goat and rabbit.

- **The Cleveland Metroparks Zoo** (3900 Wildlife Way, Cleveland, 216-661-6500, www.clemetzoo.com) is a wonderful outing for adults as well as children. The zoo is spread out over 183 hilly acres so take your walking shoes if you want to see the nearly three thousand animals. One of the top attractions is the Rain-Forest, a gigantic building that replicates a tropical rain forest.

- **The Rock and Roll Hall of Fame and Museum** (1100 Rock and Roll Boulevard, Cleveland, 216-781-7625, www.rockhall.com) features 150,000 square feet of ever-changing exhibits and theaters over seven floors. The museum is located right on Lake Erie.

- **The Cleveland Museum of Art** (11150 East Boulevard, Cleveland, 216-421-7340, www.clevelandart.org) is free. Yes, free. The museum features more than forty thousand objects spanning six thousand years.

- **Lola** (2058 E. Fourth Street, Cleveland, 216-621-5652, www.lolabistro .com) and **Lolita** (900 Literary Road, Cleveland, 216-771-5652). If you're into specialty dining, you will be glad to know that Michael Symon, the famous chef who's featured on the Food Network, has two restaurants in the area.

- **Melt Bar & Grilled** (www.meltbarandgrilled.com), a restaurant that specializes in big cheesy meals, has been featured on the Travel Channel and Food Network, and its owner Matt Fish was named one of *Cleveland Magazine*'s most interesting people in 2010. The restaurant has two locations: 14718 Detroit Avenue, Lakewood, 216-226-3699; and 13463 Cedar Road, Cleveland Heights, 216-965-0988.

- **Little Italy** (www.littleitalycleveland.com). Looking for some Italian food? Check out Little Italy, a close-knit neighborhood on the city's east side filled with restaurants and art galleries.

Black Box Brewing Company

24945 Detroit Road, Westlake, OH 44145
440-871-0700 • www.jwdover.com

Black Box Brewing Company owes its existence to a crayon. Really! Jerome Welliver had bought a homebrew and winemaking shop in 1997 and renamed it JW Dover. He had no intention of opening a brewery as part of that venture. For years, he was quite happy just running the shop and building his clientele.

Then a friend spotted a crayon-scrawled "For sale" sign on the side of the road in Mansfield in 2004. It simply said there was a brewery for sale. Intrigued, Welliver drove there to check it out.

The Wooden Pony Brewing Company had opened in Mansfield in the mid-1990s and closed by 2002. A new owner bought the building after the brewpub shut down but didn't want the brewing equipment. Welliver was able to buy the brewery on the cheap, dismantle it, and haul it to Westlake.

There was one major problem. Welliver had the money to purchase the equipment, but he did not have the money to start brewing. So the brewhouse sat unused in pieces in storage at the homebrew and winemaking shop for two years. He figured that even if he never brewed, he got a

Beers brewed: Year-round: Black Box brands are Javelin Ale and Plumbers Crack Ale. Western Reserve brands are Cloud Nine, Bockzilla, and American Wheat. Crooked River brands are Black Forest Lager, Lighthouse Gold, Cool Mule Porter, Settlers Ale ESB, and Irish Red Ale. There also are seasonal beers.

The Pick: The Javelin Ale is great for malt fans. It's an American amber rye with hints of raisins and plums.

heck of a deal. Every so often, he'd walk by and just tap the equipment.

"It was cool to look at," he said. "I was intrigued by the mechanics of it. My brain works that way. My wife laughs but I like this stuff. I like the ingenuity. I like figuring things out. I like the challenge, and this was going to be a great challenge. This is going to be a lot of hard work, but hell I've got direction and we'll go from there. My homebrews were good but I never said, 'Oh I'm going to go on the market with these.'"

Welliver finally got enough money together in late 2005 to start assembling the brewhouse, and after a lengthy and frustrating approval process by local and state authorities, Black Box was brewing by late 2006. Welliver was more relieved than excited by the time the first beer was brewed.

"The excitement had worn off by then to be honest," Welliver said. "The excitement was putting it together and then the politics beat the hell out of you."

Black Box, a production brewery and not a brewpub, is located in a brick, strip-mall type building just off Interstate 90 in Westlake, a Cleveland suburb of about thirty thousand people. When visitors walk in, the only thing they see is the beer and winemaking shop. The brewhouse is in the back of the building, out of sight of customers.

Before he bought the place, Welliver visited the shop to buy ingredients for his own homebrewing. At the time, he was in the nuclear power and radiation protection industry, a job that had him traveling and away from home for at least six to nine months in a row. After ten years of that, he wanted a more stable home life. One day, he walked into the shop and noticed that the owner was miserable.

"I'm like, 'Dude my job kinda sucks right now traveling all the time, but if it sucked as bad as yours looks to be to you, I wouldn't be doing it.' And he smart-ass commented me back, 'It's for sale if you want it, smart-ass.' And I went, 'Oh, okay.'"

Welliver started checking out different homebrew shops but loved the history of the Westlake location, which had been open since 1928 and started as a farmer's co-op. The shop sells everything you'd expect at a homebrew and winemaking business. There are different grains, beer and wine kits, yeasts, equipment, and how-to books.

Cleveland-area beer drinkers might recognize Welliver's name and just not remember why. Well, he was co-host of *Beer Talk Radio*, a local show that ran for six years. He was on the program for more than four years. He loved that opportunity, saying it was incredible to be able to talk with such brewing icons as August Busch III of Anheuser-Busch, Fritz Maytag of Anchor Brewing, and Jim Koch of Boston Beer, as well as all the local talent in the Cleveland beer scene.

When it comes to Black Box, the beer mirrors Welliver's personal taste. He's interested in session beers and not high-alcohol, crazy beers. But he's also not afraid to experiment. He created Cucumber Wheat in 2010 for the Pawpaw Festival in southern Ohio. The unusual light beer was made with real, handpicked Ohio-grown cucumbers and has a slight cucumber aftertaste.

Black Box also brews the Western Reserve and Crooked River line-up of beers. Both those Cleveland breweries went belly up, but Welliver became part of an investment team that acquired both brands.

"We are very big on quality," Welliver said. "Of course, everybody is worried about quality. We live quality. If things just aren't right, we're not putting the beer out. We don't care. We're not on a time schedule here. We're not thumbs to the wall having to make a profit so therefore we must cut corners. We give the people what they expect. I don't lie to people. I don't pull their legs. I tell them what's what. It's a great opportunity to have a well-crafted beer."

Black Box Brewing Company

Opened: The beer and winemaking shop opened in 1997. Black Box Brewing started in 2006.

Owner: Jerome Welliver.

Brewers: Jerome Welliver and Tom Gray.

System: 10-barrel Criveller system.

Production: 1,320 barrels.

Distribution: Cuyahoga County.

Hours: The homebrew and winemaking shop is open Tuesday, 10 A.M. to 8 P.M.; Wednesday, Thursday, and Friday, 10 A.M. to 6 P.M.; and Saturday, 10 A.M. to 4 P.M.

Tours: Upon request during the week from noon to 5 P.M.

Take-out beer: Growlers, six-packs, and kegs.

Extras: The business offers homebrew and winemaking supplies, as well as beer.

Parking: There is a large parking lot outside the business.

Other area beer sites: See page 18.

The Brew Kettle Taproom & Smokehouse

8377 Pearl Road, Strongsville, OH 44136
440-239-8788 • www.thebrewkettle.com

The Brew Kettle owner, Chris McKim, knew he could make it in the beer industry after delivering tap handles to a local bar that was serving one of his first batches of beer.

"Somebody right down the bar from me, who didn't know me from Adam, ordered one of our beers and was talking to his buddy about how good it was," he recalled. "And I thought, 'I think I can make this work.' It was really a cool thing. It was something you'll never forget."

That was 1995. McKim had left his successful job as a sales manager in the automotive industry to start his own brewery and the state's first brew-on-premises operation in Strongsville, a Cleveland suburb of about forty-five thousand people.

A year earlier, McKim was in Costa Rica on vacation when some people from Vancouver told him about the brew-on-premises industry in Canada. A brew-on-premises involves people coming to your business and making their own beer there under the guidance of a professional brewer. People pay a little more than they would if they brewed at home, but it's seen as a social event—and in Canada, a way to get around high beer taxes.

McKim was intrigued. He took a few trips to Canada to make beer at one of the locations and see what it was all about. He figured he could do that. So he opened not only a brew-on-premises business, but also a brewery and barbecue restaurant. The first few years, he said, the business struggled and he worked one hundred hours a week without drawing a paycheck. McKim, who was a homebrewer but had no previous restaurant experience, served as owner, brewer, and delivery boy.

The Brew Kettle grew slowly and now is a thriving operation with about seventy-five employees. The business has greatly expanded over the years. The Brew Kettle occupies a one-story, strip mall–type building along busy Pearl Road. The location houses the brew-on-premises business, restaurant, a distillery, and a make-your-own wine shop.

Beers brewed: Year-round: Big Woody, Copperhead Red, Four C's Pale Ale, and Red Eye PA. There also are many seasonal and rotating beers available.

The Pick: The Red Eye PA won a silver medal at the 2010 Great American Beer Festival. It's a highly hopped amber ale that hopheads will love.

The production brewery moved a few miles down the road in 2007 into an industrial park. That's also where the corporate offices are and all the meat for the restaurant is smoked there in a hickory smoker.

In the beginning, McKim marketed his own beer under the name Ringneck Brewing Company, because he was concerned that bar and restaurant owners wouldn't want to put a beer from a competing restaurant on their menu. He's since retired Ringneck, saying it was confusing for customers who wondered what the difference was between Ringneck and The Brew Kettle.

The brew-on-premises operation, with its eight mini kettles, is located in the back of the brewpub. For some reason, the business has taken off, McKim said. The waiting list for appointments is several months long, even longer for a Saturday.

The brewpub itself is small. Before a major expansion in 2010, it was just a long, skinny place with a bar on one wall and booths on the other. The expansion added seventy-five seats, but it still feels small and intimate.

There's an impressive collection of breweriana on the walls, including trays, signs, tap handles, bottles, and posters. They sport names from long-ago beers like Monarch, Ortlieb's, Krueger, Old Shay, Cinci Cream, and Piels.

The Brew Kettle offers thirty beers on tap—both house and guest beers. McKim has no qualms about selling his beer alongside the best that the craft industry has to offer. He has since retired as the brewer, handing over the reins to Jack Kephart, a former brewer at the Willoughby Brewing Company.

In 2010, The Brew Kettle took home two medals at the Great American Beer Festival: a silver for its Red Eye PA, a highly hopped amber ale; and a bronze for Jack Hammer, a barleywine. The medals, which hang on both sides of his computer monitor in his office, are great validation for all the hard work, McKim said.

The Brew Kettle must be doing something right with the beer and atmosphere. Ratebeer.com has named The Brew Kettle as one of the best brewpubs in the United States in its annual rankings.

"We obviously are not a franchise," McKim said. "I didn't try to make this into a Friday's with a brewery in it. I just wanted it to be a pub."

The music is almost never loud and people tend to talk more at The Brew Kettle. McKim described his place as "a very talky bar. It's pubbier than most bars." He then laughed and admitted that "pubbier" isn't a word. Many cookie-cutter chain restaurants want to get customers their beer and food quickly and then hustle them out to make room for the next batch of customers. The Brew Kettle doesn't operate that way.

"I don't care if they stay all night as long as they're having fun and talking and enjoying it," McKim said.

He also prides himself on hiring knowledgeable workers. He wants people who know about beer and can carry on a conversation with customers.

"We try to hire the best people that we can find," McKim said. "We don't hire kids to do the work. If you walk in and have a question about beer, I want the guy you're asking the question to look like somebody you can trust with the answer."

The Brew Kettle Taproom & Smokehouse

Opened: 1995.

Owners: Chris and Pam McKim.

Brewer: Jack Kephart.

System: 20-barrel Specific Mechanical system.

Production: 1,000 barrels at the production brewery and 2,000 at the brew-on-premises site.

Distribution: Ohio.

Hours: Monday through Thursday, 11:30 A.M. to 11 P.M.; Friday and Saturday, 11:30 A.M. to midnight; Sunday, 1 P.M. to 9 P.M.

Tours: Upon request.

Food: The Brew Kettle specializes in hickory-smoked barbecue, like ribs and pulled pork. The menu ranges from typical bar appetizers and burgers to more creative entrees, such as chicken Parma-que and barbecued spaghetti.

Extras: There's much more to the Brew Kettle than just a brewpub; there's also a brew-on-premises business, distillery, and make-your-own wine shop.

Take-out beer: Growlers, 22-ounce bottles, and kegs.

Parking: There is a large parking lot in front of the business.

Other area beer sites: See page 18.

Buckeye Brewing Company / Beer Engine

15315 Madison Avenue, Lakewood, OH 44107
216-226-2337 • buckeyebrewing.com
buckeyebeerengine.com

Buckeye Brewing Company owner Garin Wright talks a mile a minute, and he's not afraid to share his opinion on any beer-related subject. He fully admits he's outspoken and a loudmouth.

For example, he's not happy that people tend to fawn over California and Michigan beers here. Not that he's disparaging other brands, but this is Ohio, and he wants to see more breweries open here and wants consumers to support the local craft industry.

He's also convinced that beer names are too long and too difficult for people to remember at the end of a night of drinking. They should be two syllables and that's it. Thus his beer lineup featuring names like Hippie, Bling Bling, Martian, and Zatek.

And, unlike other brewers, he doesn't mind if his 22-ounce bottles all sport different labels. Consumers may find it difficult at first to figure out that the beers were produced by the same brewery. But that's fine with him.

"We want to have more brands on the shelf because I believe one of the niches is people right now are shopping for whatever is new or they've never seen before," Wright said. "They are getting sick and tired of the same five portfolio beers that a brewery has been making for the last fifteen years. That's my opinion."

Buckeye Brewing started out in 1997 as a brew-on-premises business in Bedford Heights, an eastern suburb of Cleveland. At the time, the business was split into the Brew Keeper, which was a brew-on-premises operation, and Buckeye Brewing, which made its own brands on draft and in bottles for retail sale. Wright and his father, Robert, decided to focus solely on Buckeye and sold off the Brew Keeper in 2006.

The Wrights moved to an old manufacturing building that once housed the Industrial Rayon Corporation on the west side of Cleveland. The

Beers brewed: Year-round: Hippie IPA, Bling Bling Pale Ale, and '76 IPA. There also are rotating and seasonal beers available, including Christmas Girl.

The Pick: You can't go wrong with Hippie IPA, the beer that really put Buckeye Brewing on the map. It's an amber-colored, big hoppy beer that should delight hopheads, but not overpower them with its 6.8 percent alcohol.

majority of the building contains Ray's MTB Indoor Park, a gigantic BMX track. Interestingly enough, there's no sign indicating Buckeye Brewing is there. Just a door.

That's the way the Wrights want it. The production brewery is low-key and not open to the public. The Buckeye beer scene can be found at the Beer Engine restaurant in the nearby suburb of Lakewood. The Wrights bought a small restaurant in 2007 and transformed it into a brewpub to feature their beers and push craft beer in general.

The Beer Engine is a major beer bar. It's not big inside—about the size of a fast-food restaurant. But it's big on beer selection. All the Buckeye beers are on tap, as well as twenty-seven guest beers. The restaurant also offers an impressive list of bottled beer, with about two hundred available, ranging from Aecht Schlenkerla Marzen to Carling Black Label.

The half-moon-shaped bar dominates the room. The walls are filled with beer posters and signs. A shelf near the ceiling holds different beer bottles, and beer taps hang from the shelf.

The restaurant specializes in gourmet hamburgers and beer-related events, including a hop festival, Christmas in Belgium, and a real ale fest. The Wrights have even brought in big names in the beer industry, such as Adam Avery from Avery Brewing Company and Garrett Oliver from Brooklyn Brewing, for special beer tastings. The restaurant also held what's considered Ohio's first beer and breakfast pairing. Lines were out the door.

The Beer Engine also does something unusual for the brewpub industry. It's open from 11 A.M. to 2:30 A.M. every day of the year. Even holidays! Wright said it's important to be open for beer fans all the time and he doesn't want to shut down the restaurant.

As for Buckeye Brewing, Wright made his name in the craft beer industry by concentrating on hoppy beers. Buckeye offers only three year-round beers: Hippie, Bling Bling, and '76. All three are hoppy. Hippie, first released in 1998, was considered the hoppiest Ohio-made beer at the time. And this was back before IPAs were fashionable in the state.

"Now people don't even consider it an IPA, but at the time it was the hoppiest beer in Cleveland, if not Ohio," Wright said. "To this day it's considered our flagship beer."

Buckeye Brewing picked up plenty of publicity in 2010 when it released Witless, a jab at former Cleveland Cavs player LeBron James, who bolted to the Miami Heat as a free agent. The Witless name was a play on the famous Nike campaign that urged people to "Witness" James's greatness. The beer itself—suggested by Ed Thompkins, the beer and wine buyer for the Heinen's grocery chain—was a Belgian-style wheat beer brewed with orange peel and coriander. The label touted Wright's affinity for Cleveland: "Lose the King, gain a beer! This sudsy tribute was brewed to celebrate the fierce pride and loyalty we have for our fair city."

Early on, Wright opted to sell his beer in 22-ounce bottles and still does. Up until 2010, the brewery still bottled by hand, one bottle at a time. Since, the company has invested in a machine that can fill two bottles at a time. Buckeye Brewing has plans to offer six-packs in 12-ounce bottles, but Wright still believes in and will sell the bigger bottles.

"The consumer doesn't have to make the choice to buy a whole six-pack," he said. "They can see a nice array of beers on the shelf and say, 'Alright I'll try this. It's only one bottle.' The other reason is because on the shelf there's more surface area and you can do a lot more with the artwork. It's not shoved into a six-pack carrier. It's in front of your face."

And as Wright will tell you, he wants Buckeye Beer to be in your face.

Buckeye Brewing Company / Beer Engine

Opened: 1997.

Owners: Garin Wright and Robert Wright.

Brewer: Garin Wright.

System: 15-barrel Century system.

Production: More than 1,000 barrels.

Distribution: Ohio.

Hours: The Beer Engine is open daily, 11 A.M. to 2:30 A.M., even holidays. The production brewery isn't open to the public.

Tours: Upon request.

Take-out beer: Growlers.

Food: The Beer Engine specializes in gourmet hamburgers, but also serves other sandwiches.

Extras: The brewpub hosts numerous special events throughout the year, ranging from a Belgian beer festival to industry leaders coming in to share a beer with customers. Sign up for Garin's e-mail newsletter at the website for details about upcoming events.

Parking: There is a small parking lot at the Beer Engine.

Other area beer sites: See page 18.

Cleveland ChopHouse & Brewery

824 W. Saint Clair Avenue, Cleveland, OH 44113
(216) 623-0909 • www.clevelandchophouse.com

The Cleveland ChopHouse has no cute or quirky names for its beers like those that dominate the lineups at other brewpubs. The light beer is called Light Lager. The Irish red ale is Irish Red. The pilsner—a two-time winner at the Great American Beer Festival—is simply Bohemian Pilsner. The stout is . . . well, you get the idea.

They're just working-class names for a working-class city. But it's odd given the Cleveland ChopHouse atmosphere, which is much more casual steakhouse than down-and-dirty bar. You would think the clientele, made up of a lot of professionals, would embrace a funky name or two.

The brewpub is decidedly more restaurant than bar, with the vast majority of space devoted to dining. The long bar even sits away from the main dining area. The brewhouse and fermenters are housed behind glass, just like they are in most brewpubs.

The bar does have an unusual feature—at least for an Ohio brewpub. An ice rail runs the length of the bar. What's an ice rail? It's a piece of frozen metal set into the bar top. People can set their beer or other drinks on it to keep them cold. The ice rail works wonders for people who are more interested in enjoying their beer than chugging it.

"It's a novelty as much as anything," said brewer Gerry OConnell (yes, his last name has no apostrophe). "But it is impressive."

The Cleveland ChopHouse, which is owned by the same company that operates both the Rock Bottom and Gordon Biersch chains, is in the city's Warehouse District downtown. The area is filled with niche restaurants and bars in converted warehouses. It's not unusual to see valets parking cars. Many of the historic brick buildings also contain offices, condominiums, and lofts, meaning there are always people milling about.

The brewpub is right around the corner from Cleveland Browns Stadium. The Cleveland ChopHouse takes full advantage of the proximity by holding a Sunday brunch, and Browns fans descend upon the place en masse.

Beers brewed: Year-round: Light Lager, Bohemian Pilsner, American Wheat, Irish Red, and Irish Stout. The brewery also has four or five rotating and seasonal beers.

The Pick: The Bohemian Pilsner won two gold medals at the Great American Beer Festival. The straw-colored beer is a light, clean lawnmower beer. It's hard not to pick that.

Cleveland's party district used to be in the nearby Flats district along the Cuyahoga River. But partygoers migrated to the Warehouse District as the Flats died out. The Flats also was home to a Rock Bottom restaurant at one time, but it closed in 2010. The Cleveland Chop-House has plenty of unused capacity and there were plans to start brewing some beer for the Cincinnati Rock Bottom because of how successful that location has become.

"Cleveland's a pretty good beer town. I was impressed," said OConnell, a native of Tralee, Ireland, who moved to the United States in 1994. "There are a lot of good little brewpubs here."

OConnell enjoys a lot of brewing freedom. There are no corporate mandates on what he has to make. The company wants its brewers to make what the people in that community want to drink.

OConnell, who grew up on a dairy farm, fell into the brewing business by accident. When he moved to the United States, he started working in the kitchen at the Brew Moon Brewery in Boston. The company decided to open a bunch of restaurants in a short time period and he was able to get a job as an assistant brewer. He later became the head brewer at one of the sites.

"Right time, right place," OConnell said. Rock Bottom eventually bought out Brew Moon. And when his Rock Bottom brewpub was closed in Boston, he decided to transfer to Cleveland.

Asked to describe the difference between beer drinkers in Ireland and the United States, OConnell said there are more options here. There are a few brewpubs in Ireland, but in general people drink Guinness and Heineken, he said.

The Cleveland ChopHouse has six beers in its regular lineup, and they are the ones you'd expect at any brewpub, such as a pilsner and stout. But OConnell also has four or five rotating and seasonal beers on tap all the time. His personal favorite is pilsner and he was psyched to come to a brewpub with a history of making one of the best in the country.

"Classic beers are classic for a reason," OConnell said. "It's great fun to brew a Scotch ale but when you go out having a couple of beers, I like the session beers."

Not that beer drinkers will find only a pilsner and other session beers on the beer menu. OConnell isn't afraid to make such high-alcohol favorites as a barrel-aged stout.

"The great thing about the brewpub is you can pretty much brew whatever the hell you want," he said. "With eleven beers, that's a pretty good lineup."

Cleveland ChopHouse & Brewery

Opened: 1998.

Owner: CraftWorks Restaurants & Breweries.

Brewer: Gerry OConnell.

System: 10-barrel JV Northwest.

Production: 500 barrels.

Distribution: At the brewpub only.

Hours: Monday through Thursday, 11:30 A.M. to 10 P.M.; Friday and Saturday, 11:30 A.M. to 11 P.M.; Sunday, 10 A.M. to 2 P.M. for brunch.

Tours: Upon request.

Take-out beer: Growlers and kegs.

Food: The Cleveland ChopHouse is a casual steakhouse, so the menu is filled with plenty of steaks and seafood.

Extras: The ChopHouse has a wine club and offers wine dinners and tastings, as well as beer-pairing dinners with the brewer.

Parking: On-street parking and parking lots.

Other area beer sites: See page 18.

Cornerstone Brewing Company

58 Front Street, Berea, OH 44017
440-239-9820
70 and 74 W. Main Street, Madison, OH 44057
440-983-4520 • www.cornerstonebrewing.com

Most brewpubs have a stable of regular beers and offer a seasonal here and there. Cornerstone Brewing does it a bit differently. Only three beers are mainstays on tap, and they are ones you'd expect to find at any brewpub: light lager, amber ale, and India pale ale.

But Cornerstone offers much more than three house beers. It has nine taps devoted to its brews, leaving six rotating beers. Well-known seasonals, such as pumpkin and Christmas beers, pop up, as do brown ales and fruit beers. Anything could show up on the beer menu one day, stick around for a little while, and then disappear.

That setup suits brewer Jay Cox just fine, providing him with great flexibility to be creative and not fall into any rut. It's also great for regular craft beer drinkers who are always looking for variety and something new. If he wants to experiment with buckwheat, for example, he can—and has.

"I love the fact that we have so many tap lines for the simple fact that you can do whatever," Cox said. "I always try to have something different available. I hate going into some place and seeing the same things on tap."

That penchant for experimentation even extends to one of the regular beers. Cox, who grew up in Syracuse and has a background in computer animation, will occasionally tweak the India pale ale, simply known as Seven, in an attempt to mix it up.

"I like everything. I want to brew everything," he said when asked about his brewing style.

Cornerstone was founded in 2004 by Roy Blalock. He took over the site of the former Quarryman Tavern & Brewery. The Cornerstone name fits for a couple of reasons. First, the brewpub sits in a corner brick building in downtown Berea. And second, the community became famous years ago for its rock quarries and grindstones.

Today, the town—located only twenty minutes from downtown Cleveland—is better known to many as the home of the Cuyahoga County Fairgrounds, training camp for the NFL's Cleveland Browns, and Baldwin-Wallace College, a liberal arts college with about forty-three hundred students.

The brewpub is a small, relaxed place that receives great support from the surrounding community. There are only about ninety seats. And with only two flat-screen televisions above the small bar, the focus is more on the restaurant side of the business and socializing. The bar is granite and the kitchen, which serves casual American food, is exposed for patrons to see.

That open kitchen sets Cornerstone apart from many other restaurants and brewpubs. People get to see the food being made and there's more interaction with the chefs.

Cornerstone opened a second location in 2009 along the main street in downtown Madison, a small village in Lake County about an hour east of Berea. The Madison restaurant is similar—both in the exterior brick building and the décor and atmosphere inside. There are two major differences, though. There's no exposed kitchen in Madison

Beers brewed: Year-round beers: Grindstone Gold; Sandstone, a marzen; and Seven, an India pale ale. Cornerstone also has six taps devoted to seasonal beers that include a wheat, Oktoberfest, pumpkin, amber ale, hefeweizen, and Christmas.

The Pick: Considering there are only three regular beers and that the beer menu is constantly changing, it's really tough to single out one. But try the best seller, Grindstone Gold, a clean and crisp American-style lager.

and no brewhouse. The beer is made in Berea and then shipped to the Madison restaurant.

There's a difference in tastes between the two locations, as well. For some reason, folks in Madison have a strong desire for dark beers, such as porters, even during the heat of summer.

"They are constantly jonesing for them," Cox said. "And I don't know why."

Believe it or not, Cox works two full-time jobs. In addition to brewing at Cornerstone, which he focuses on during the weekends, he also does video production for the Summit County Board of Developmental Disabilities, creating commercials, public-service announcements, and training videos.

"I'm lucky enough to have two jobs I love doing," Cox said. "I'm making beer and I'm making videos. Both jobs are exceedingly creative."

Cornerstone Brewing Company

Opened: 2004. The second location opened in 2009.

Owner: Roy Blalock.

Brewer: Jay Cox.

System: 15-barrel Pub Brewing system.

Production: More than 500 barrels.

Distribution: At the brewpubs only.

Hours: The kitchen at both sites is open Monday through Thursday, 11:30 A.M. to 10 P.M.; Friday, 11:30 A.M. to 11 P.M.; and Saturday, noon to 11 P.M. On Sunday, the Berea site is open 1 P.M. to 9 P.M., but the Madison restaurant is closed. The bars at both Cornerstones are open later than the kitchen and there's no set closing time.

Tours: Upon request.

Take-out beer: Growlers.

Food: Cornerstone offers a full menu ranging from appetizers and salads to burgers and pizzas. There also are many dinner entrees, including chicken Diablo, bacon-wrapped sirloin, and Sante Fe salmon.

Parking: On street at both locations.

Other area beer sites: See page 18.

Fat Head's Brewery & Saloon

24581 Lorain Road, North Olmsted, OH 44070
440-801-1001 • www.fatheadscleveland.com

Many brewers have a science or engineering background, which certainly helps in the brewing process or even in building a brewery. Matt Cole, one of the most decorated and respected brewers in Ohio, has neither. He graduated from the University of Pittsburgh with a degree in criminal justice.

"I've stayed out of jail," he joked. "I think I'm more of the crafty, artistic side of it and have forced myself to learn the applied sciences. You don't have to be a microbiologist on a level like this to run a nice, tight brewery."

The crafty, artsy side has served him well. Cole, who previously worked for the Rocky River, Great Lakes, and Baltimore breweries, has racked up plenty of awards for his recipes, including numerous medals at the Great American Beer Festival. That trend continued when Fat Head's Brewery & Saloon opened in 2009 in North Olmsted, a suburb of about thirty-four thousand people on the west side of Cleveland.

The brewpub's Head Hunter IPA has been named one of the best twenty-five beers in the world by *Draft Magazine*. Head Hunter also has picked up a silver medal at the Great American Beer Festival, a gold at the West Coast IPA Festival, and gold at the annual National IPA Championship sponsored by the *Brewing News*. The Bumbleberry Honey Blueberry Ale also won the industry newspaper's Global Warming Open competition.

Fat Head's is in a standalone retail building along busy Lorain Road. The building once housed a gourmet farmer's market called Danny Boy's. The space is huge and has high-vaulted ceilings and exposed brick. With 13,000 square feet, there's plenty of room for a large bar area, dining area with wooden booths and live plants, game room with pool tables and dart boards, a gift shop selling T-shirts and hats, and of course, the brewery, which is visible through glass in the bar area.

Beers brewed: Year-round: Starlight Lager, Duke of Lager, Bumbleberry Honey Blueberry Ale, Head Hunter IPA, and Gogglefogger. There usually are eight to twelve house beers on tap, so there are many rotating and seasonal beers available.

The Pick: The Head Hunter IPA has garnered so many accolades it'd be silly to select something else. It's a highly hopped yet remarkably smooth West Coast IPA. The menu description sums it up perfectly: "uncivilized and aggressive."

The top of the bar is made of concrete with colorful glass mixed in; it's large and provides plenty of seating for folks who just want to drink the beer as opposed to eat lunch or dinner. Etched in wood behind the bar is the phrase, "One big hoppy family." The Fat Head's logo—a big fat guy with a double chin—is everywhere. Logos from other breweries such as Great Lakes, Victory, and Sierra Nevada also are painted on the brick walls. Framed beer medals are mounted on the walls in the bar area and large banners noting the *Brewing News* wins hang down over the bar itself.

"It's a casual, rustic atmosphere," co-owner Paul Siperke said. "We're not a fancy place."

The owners, who strived to make Fat Head's family friendly, even paid tribute to the past by dedicating a wall to Danny Boy's. There, you'll find an old sign and many photos of what the building and space used to look like. Everybody on Cleveland's west side knew about Danny Boy's and many worked there growing up.

Cole, who also is one of the owners, and Siperke said the community was disappointed when the farmer's market closed. The building had been vacant for a couple of years before Fat Head's moved in. North Olmsted was craving a non-chain restaurant, they said. While Fat Head's isn't a chain, per se, it is a franchise. The original Fat Head's is in Pittsburgh, but that location isn't a brewery. The North Olmsted brewpub supplies beer to the Pittsburgh restaurant, though. Both locations are known for their Headwiches, a name for their sandwiches, because they are supposed to be as big as your head.

With the success of Head Hunter, Fat Head's has quickly earned a following among IPA fans. The brewpub also hosts an annual IPA festival in October that attracts breweries from around the country. In May, the brewpub also holds the Heavyweight Brewer's Brawl, a festival featuring big beers.

As for the Fat Head's beer, Cole loves to research beer styles. That involves traveling to California and Europe to sample the best that the world has to offer.

"I'm not out there trying to steal people's recipes," he said. "I'm trying to learn what makes their beer so good. A lot of guys don't do that. What we strive for here is beers that are very crisp and clean, and I'll use the term dangerously drinkable. We work hard on our water. We ferment our beers cooler than a lot of people do, which makes them less fruity and a little crisper. We give our beers lengthy periods of conditioning so they are rounded. We don't filter beer. I strongly believe that filtration strips out color, body, mouthfeel, bitterness and is very detrimental to aromatics."

Fat Head's has anywhere from eight to twelve house beers on tap at any given time. There are only five mainstays on the beer menu, so there's always a new rotating or seasonal beer available. The brewpub offers more than its own beer, too. There are about twenty-four guest beers designed to fill in any gaps in beer styles not represented by the Fat Head's brands.

The brewpub also began bottling its beer in late 2010 on a limited basis. Because of the popularity of Head Hunter, Fat Head's planned to make that available in bottles. Don't expect to see the beer in grocery stores immediately, though. Cole said it would be available at the brewpub and possibly some specialty beer stores in the area.

Fat Head's Brewery & Saloon

Opened: 2009.

Owners: Matt Cole, Paul Siperke, Danny Douglass, Derek Wilson, and Ted Lipovan.

Brewer: Matt Cole

System: A 10-barrel JV Northwest system, which originally was built for Miller Brewing Company for a Leinenkugel brewpub.

Production: 1,600 barrels.

Distribution: At the brewpub only.

Hours: Sunday through Wednesday, 11 A.M. to midnight; and Thursday through Saturday, 11 A.M. to 1 A.M.

Tours: Upon request.

Take-out beer: Growlers, kegs, and some bottles.

Food: The menu ranges from burgers to pizza to wings. But Fat Head's is best known for its Headwiches, so named because they are supposed to be the size of a human head. The Headwiches come with comical names like Beauty & the Beasty (pulled pork topped with cole slaw, pickles, and raw onions) and The Full Cleveland (kielbasa and brats topped with hot-pepper kraut, melted Swiss, Thousand Island, and Stadium Mustard).

Extras: Fat Head's has a mug club. The mugs are kept behind the bar in a huge wall filled with cubbyholes.

Parking: There is a large lot in the back of the building.

Other area beer sites: See page 18.

Great Lakes Brewing Company

2516 Market Avenue, Cleveland, OH 44113
216-771-4404 • www.greatlakesbrewing.com

When Patrick and Daniel Conway dreamed about opening a brewery in the mid-1980s, they wanted it to be part of a renaissance in Cleveland. The Conways were raised in the city and loved the community; they didn't want to see their brewery tucked away in a suburb.

They chose the Ohio City neighborhood in downtown's near west side for their fledgling operation. Some thought they were crazy. At the time, Ohio City was a gritty, urban area struggling with crime despite being home to two longtime, positive community institutions: the West Side Market and St. Ignatius High School.

Great Lakes Brewing Company was born in 1988 on a small street—more like an alleyway—between the market and the high school. No one realized it at the time, but the brewery would help spawn a rebirth in the neighborhood and pave the way for the start of the craft beer revolution in Ohio. Today, Great Lakes, the second-oldest operating brewery in the state outside of the Anheuser-Busch InBev plant in Columbus, is revered nationwide not only for the quality of its beer but also for its civic leadership and positive portrayal of Cleveland.

"We've certainly brought the spotlight to our city because one of the best breweries in the country is right here in Ohio City," co-owner Patrick Conway said.

For the Conways, Great Lakes is more than just brewing beer. The company has adopted a triple bottom-line business philosophy that recognizes the financial, social, and environmental impacts of decisions. Efforts range from supporting nonprofit organizations, organically growing food for the brewpub at a nearby urban garden, and installing solar panels atop the roof to preheat the water used in the brewing process.

Beers brewed: Year-round: Dortmunder Gold Lager, Eliot Ness Amber Lager, Edmund Fitzgerald Porter, Burning River Pale Ale, and Commodore Perry IPA. The brewery also offers rotating and seasonal beers, including the classic Christmas Ale.

The Pick: This is difficult because everything Great Lakes makes is outstanding. If you can, try the Christmas Ale, which is brewed with honey and spiced with fresh ginger and cinnamon. Around Ohio, every brewer compares his Christmas beer to Christmas Ale. If that is out of season, the Edmund Fitzgerald Porter is a complex brew with roasted chocolate-coffee flavor. It's won fifteen medals through the years at the Great American Beer Festival, World Beer Cup, and World Beer Championships.

"The whole paradigm of 'take, make, waste' is blown up and redirected into 'take, make, remake,'" Patrick Conway said. "The entire philosophy of our company is to find and implement higher and better uses of our waste. I think our customers are celebrating this paradigm shift with us. Many companies are a flash in the pan these days. Our aspirations lay beyond the profits. Great Lakes is a brand that people love and support above and beyond the award-winning beer. Our customers want to support us for what we believe and execute as a company and what we stand for in the community."

For a few reasons, including the neighborhood, it's amazing that Great Lakes survived while so many other craft brewers from the 1980s and 1990s went out of business. The Conways had no brewing or restaurant experience before starting the company: Patrick was a social studies teacher and Daniel was a loan officer. They knew they needed help to launch their venture. So Patrick let his fingers do the walking and looked in the phone book under "B" for brewers. The only thing he found was a listing for a soft drink union. He called anyway and asked if they knew any brewers who could help.

They hooked Patrick up with master brewer Thaine Johnson and engineer Charlie Price, who both had three decades of brewing experience and had worked at the city's last production brewery, Christian Schmidt. Johnson and Price thought the Great Lakes system was "cute," because it was so small compared to the huge systems they previously worked on. Patrick Conway credits Johnson and Price with getting the brewery off to a successful start.

Great Lakes has built a solid reputation and won a ton of beer medals because of its "obsession with quality." Each bottle and package features a customer-friendly freshness date (down to the day); some breweries don't put a date or only put a month on their packaging. "For our unpasteurized beers, the changes that can happen between the beginning of a month and the end of a month can be telling, which is why we drill down our freshness dates to the exact day," Patrick Conway said.

All of the Great Lakes beers are solid sellers, with Dortmunder Gold Lager leading the way.

"Our flagship is more like a fleet," Patrick Conway said, repeating the company's slogan. "We don't lead with one particular beer. We go into a market with our family of beers and let the market say what particular beer it prefers. The Edmund Fitzgerald Porter is more popular in Michigan. The Eliot Ness Amber Lager is more popular in Pittsburgh. The Burning River Pale Ale and Dortmunder Gold are doing well in Chicago. Each market has its own taste."

Considering Great Lakes now produces about one hundred thousand barrels a year and is a major tourist attraction, the brewpub still is relatively small inside. The dining and bar area is intimate and can easily get crowded. The Conways created a beer garden with an eco-friendly radiant fireplace and retractable roof to add more year-round seating and space. During the summer, people can eat outside at tables along the tree-lined avenue.

The brewpub features two bars: an antique tiger mahogany bar in the upstairs Taproom and a smaller one in the downstairs Beer Cellar (which feels like a "rathskeller"). The brewery's many medals from the Great American Beer Festival are framed and hang in the Taproom.

The tiger mahogany bar serves as a major conversation piece, because it has bullet holes rumored to have come from the gun of Eliot Ness, the legendary crime fighter who led a group of law-enforcement agents known as "The Untouchables" in Chicago. The brewpub sits in a series of row buildings that once housed a hotel, feed company, livery stable, and a tavern that was frequented by Ness when he served as Cleveland's safety director.

Diners and visitors can walk from the brewpub into the largest brewery retail shop in the state. The shop sells not only Great Lakes beer, but everything else imaginable, including golf balls, beer soap, and framed posters.

Great Lakes has two separate brewhouses. The original seven-barrel system sits behind glass in the brewpub and is readily visible to restaurant-goers. Brewers still make some pub-exclusive beers with this system. The large production brewery is across the street and is open for weekend tours that show off the large brewhouse, stainless steel fermenters, bottling and packaging lines, and chemical and microbiological labs.

"It's important for people to know that we take a lot of pride in being Cleveland's brewery," Patrick Conway said. "We know this area is a depressed part of the economy and the country. We're losing jobs, young people, and businesses. We've put our flag in the ground and declared, 'This is our brewery and this is our town.' We want to represent our community in a positive way."

Great Lakes Brewing Company

Opened: 1988.
Owners: Patrick and Daniel Conway.
Brewer: Mark Hunger.

System: 7-barrel Century for the brewpub and a 75-barrel Mueller system for the production brewery.

Production: 100,000 barrels.

Distribution: Ohio, Indiana, Illinois, Kentucky, Michigan, Minnesota, New Jersey, New York, North Carolina, Pennsylvania, West Virginia, Wisconsin, and Washington, D.C.

Hours: Monday through Thursday, 11:30 A.M. to midnight; Friday and Saturday, 11:30 A.M. to 1 A.M. Closed Sunday.

Tours: Public tours are available on Friday from 5 P.M. to 9 P.M. and Saturday from 1 P.M. to 8 P.M.

Take-out beer: Growlers, six-packs, and sixtels.

Extras: The brewery not only offers public tours, but it also has regular beer tastings and talks, brewmaster dinners, and a private beer school. Check out the brewery website for availability. There's also a Great Lakes pub at Cleveland's Hopkins International Airport. The pub isn't owned by the brewery, but serves Great Lakes beer exclusively.

Parking: On-street parking and a public lot next door.

Other area beer sites: See page 18.

Indigo Imp Brewery

3615 Superior Avenue, Suite 4201B, Cleveland, OH 44114
216-881-0650 • www.indigoimpbrewing.com

When Matt and Kathy Chappel decided to open their own production brewery, they looked for something to make the beer stand out among all the others crowding the grocery and specialty beer store aisles. They succeeded— both in the way the beer is made and how it's packaged.

Indigo Imp uses open fermentation, a process that's unique to Ohio for a commercial brewery and rare among brewers in the United States. The vast majority of brewers ferment their beer in enclosed stainless steel vats. This lets them control the process and provide more consistency from one batch to the next.

Open fermentation, though, involves exposing the soon-to-be beer to the air. It's the way many traditional Belgian breweries make their beer, and it's more in line with how beer was made hundreds of years ago. So what's so unusual? Well, wild yeast and bacteria can jump right in and affect the flavor. Today, brewers try hard to keep wild yeast away from their beer, but those using open fermentation embrace it.

"To do the open fermentation was a fun brewing method for me," Matt said. "It also offered some unique flavors for people who had never tasted those Belgian-style beers. I think we've created some flavors that are unique to us and are not really copying somebody else's style."

With the extreme temperature changes from summer to winter—temperature affects how yeast reacts—he can tell a slight difference between the same beer packaged in a different season.

"But we do believe it still tastes like the same beer in general and it's not so crazy-different that people aren't going to believe it's the same beer in the same bottle," Matt said. "We do try to educate our customers and fans about that. If we brew a batch, the first batch for the summer, and it's a little different, I try to blog about it and say, 'This is what I noticed. This is what's a little different about it. Check it out.' And hopefully people are actually kind of interested in that. Almost the way a vintage of wine would be different from the previous year."

Indigo Imp also doesn't filter its beer, so it's cloudy. And the beer is bottle-conditioned, meaning the carbonation process takes place in the bottle and leaves a layer of sediment at the bottom.

Indigo Imp, which is a production brewery and not a brewpub, opened in December 2008 in the former W. S. Tyler Company complex on the far east side of downtown Cleveland. At one time, the company made wire cloth there.

The brick complex, now known as Tyler Village, is massive, covering 10 acres and 1.2 million square feet in several buildings. Some of the buildings date back to the 1890s. They have been renovated and now house a variety of companies, including a recording studio, television studio, artists, and furniture makers.

The brewery, which both bottles and kegs its beer, can be found on the first floor of one of those buildings. The interior is open and the Chappels haven't done much updating. The windows are the giant kind you'd expect to find in an old factory.

Matt Chappel, who was in the manufacturing industry, built a custom-made brewhouse. The operation is small. Indigo Imp has only two employees: Matt and Kathy. And Kathy has a full-time job elsewhere.

The Indigo Imp name and logo stems from their hometown. The Chappels live in Independence, a Cleveland suburb, and the school district mascot is a blue devil.

Beers brewed: Year-round: Blonde Bombshell, Jester, and Gatekeeper. The brewery also offers seasonal and rotating beers.

The Pick: The Jester is a pale ale fermented with Belgian-style yeast, giving it a different clove and slight banana flavor for a pale ale. It also has only a little hop bitterness.

"We felt it was a fun connection to the past, I guess," Matt said.

In an effort to connect more with customers, Indigo Imp began opening the brewery once a month on Friday afternoons for nonprofit fundraisers.

As for their special packaging, the Chappels hand-dip the top of one bottle from each six-pack into wax. It's a labor intensive process but has created a signature look for Indigo Imp on the store shelves. Each brand gets a different color of wax. For example, Jester, a pale ale, is dipped in red wax, while Blonde Bombshell, an American blonde ale, is dipped in blue.

The Chappels describe the beer itself as not overly hoppy like a lot of other craft beers. Instead, they try to focus on being well-balanced.

"Our style is a little different and expect that," Kathy Chappel said.

Indigo Imp Brewery

Opened: 2008.

Owners: Matt and Kathy Chappel.

Brewer: Matt Chappel.

System: Seven-barrel custom-made system.

Production: 250 barrels.

Distribution: Bars, restaurants, and grocery stores throughout Northeast Ohio.

Hours: Friday, 2:30 P.M. to 5:30 P.M. Otherwise, the production brewery isn't open to the public.

Tours: Upon request.

Take-out beer: Six-packs.

Extras: Open on Friday afternoons for nonprofit fundraisers.

Parking: There's a large parking lot outside the building.

Other area beer sites: See page 18.

Market Garden Brewery & Distillery

1947 and 1948 W. 25th Street, Cleveland, OH 44113
216-621-4000 • www.marketgardenbrewery.com

Andy Tveekrem has an impressive brewing pedigree. His first professional brewing job was with the revered Great Lakes Brewing Company, where he eventually was promoted to the level of brewmaster and helped build the company's 75-barrel brewhouse.

After that, he did a stint of contract brewing in Frederick, Maryland. That didn't work out that well because the owner of the brands he brewed ended up going through bankruptcy. It wasn't much fun wondering if your paycheck would bounce.

So Tveekrem moved on to Dogfish Head Craft Brewed Ales in Delaware, a brewery with a national reputation for high-quality beer and pushing the limits in terms of flavors and alcohol content. But he wasn't much of a fan of Delaware, where it seemed that nobody really got excited about the beer industry.

The Akron native decided to return to Northeast Ohio and open his own brewpub. Here, he said, people are enthusiastic about beer. Tveekrem, who has a history degree from the College of Wooster and did his graduate study at Kent State University, originally planned to open his brewpub in Wooster, but instead got hooked up with the owners of the Bier Markt and Bar Cento, a Belgian beer bar and restaurant in Cleveland's Ohio City neighborhood. The marriage worked well because Tveekrem did not have a restaurant background and the other partners didn't have a brewing one.

He was quite familiar with the neighborhood, because it's the home of Great Lakes Brewing. Ohio City is just across the Cuyahoga River from the heart of downtown Cleveland. It's also an area that has changed radically over the last two decades. Despite being home to two city institutions—the West Side Market and St. Ignatius High School—the community had an unsavory reputation.

The emergence of Great Lakes as a brewing mecca, the addition of places like the Bier Markt and Bar Cento, and urban housing have altered

Beers Brewed: Cluster Fuggle IPA, St. Emeric's Stout, Viking Pale Ale, and Forest City Brown Ale. With at least ten to twelve beers on tap, there are also plenty of rotating and seasonal beers.

The Pick: The Forest City Brown Ale is dark and malty, and, as the beer menu suggests, delicious and quaffable at 5.5 percent alcohol.

that perception. It's now a destination for beer lovers. Market Garden is directly across the street from the Bier Markt and Bar Cento, and next door to the West Side Market, a wonderful market that features fresh produce, meats, seafood, breads, and ethnic foods.

The brewery is in a former poultry slaughterhouse, and there are faded Chinese words and a picture of a chicken and a duck on the back of the building. That's the only hint of the building's past. The interior was gutted to the walls and a section of basement was even added.

The owners reportedly spent $3 million building the brewpub, which opened in June 2011. The brewery features two bars, chandeliers hanging in the front bar area, exposed heating and ventilation ducts on the black ceiling, dark wood floors, large fireplaces, and huge pieces of wooden art installed on a couple of the walls.

The centerpiece is the beer garden—a large outdoor patio with trees, a fireplace, and a wrought-iron gate that looks out toward the West Side Market. In addition to the beer garden, the brewpub offers outdoor dining along West 25th Street. The rooftop also is expected to be open at times.

Tveekrem was quick to point out that the beer garden won't be a German-style beer garden. People might get the wrong impression about the brewpub and think that it serves only German food, he said. The menu will showcase classic American comfort food, ranging from soups and salads to burgers, fried chicken, and bratwurst.

The Market Garden also is a separate operation from the Bier Markt, which has built a solid reputation for specializing in Belgian beers. Instead the brewpub will feature a wide range of beer styles, including the traditional brewpub staples such as a German-style lager, pale ale, wheat, and stout. Tveekrem, a beer Cicerone, planned to have at least ten to twelve house beers on tap providing beer drinkers with plenty of variety.

"If there's an emphasis I guess on our beer list, it's on having at least four or five of our beers be more sessionable, 5 percent [alcohol by volume] or less so that you can actually come in and have a few without falling off your bar stool," he said. "It's important to have that component of drinkability, approachability for people. Not approachable in terms of watered-down, bland. You know the old '90s brewpubs where you'd come in and there'd be six beers with six different colors and one same flavor. That's definitely not going to be the case."

Tveekrem is interested in producing many rotating and seasonal beers—and those with higher alcohol contents. He also plans to make some cask-conditioned beers.

"I believe in consistency and quality," he said when asked about his brewing philosophy. "I guess that's not the sexiest thing to say. I just like beer that tastes good. I figure if I like it, other people will like it. I don't try to brew for other people's tastes. I brew for my own taste and hope that I'm fairly representative of what an educated palate should be. I guess I have enough beer geek credentials to roll with that."

Market Garden Brewery & Distillery

Opened: 2011.

Owners: Andy Tveekrem, Sam McNulty, Mark Priemer, and Mike Foran.

Brewer: Andy Tveekrem.

System: 10-barrel custom-made system.

Production: An estimated 1,200 barrels

Distribution: Will be available on draft only at the brewpub, although there are plans for limited-edition bottles.

Hours: Monday through Thursday, 4 P.M. to 2:30 A.M.; Friday and Saturday, 11:30 A.M. to 2:30 A.M.; Sunday, 10 A.M. to 2:30 A.M.

Take-out beer: Growlers and limited-edition bottles.

Tours: Upon request.

Food: The menu will range from fried chicken to burgers to steak.

Extras: The word distillery is in the name for a reason. The owners plan to make their own vodka, gin, and whiskey as well.

Parking: There is a huge parking lot behind the brewpub and on-street parking along W. 25th Street.

Other area beer sites: See page 18.

Rocky River Brewing Company

21290 Center Ridge Road,
Cleveland, OH 44116
440-895-2739 • www.rockyriverbrewco.com

The Rocky River Brewing Company was designed around an old clock bought at an antiques show for $50. And not even a big grandfather clock. Just the clock face. The owners thought it looked like it was from a turn-of-the-century train station. So they mounted it above the bar and built the brewpub around it.

The brewpub features a long bar with dark wood, wooden arches, wooden floors, and exposed brick walls. A set of wooden steps leads up from the entrance to the bar and restaurant area. And as people walk up those steps, they see the clock, just as they would have in an old train station.

The bar itself is sixty feet long. That was by design.

"There were a couple of breweries we had been in prior to building this place and they all had really small bars," co-owner Gary Cintron said. "Our thing was it's a brewery. We need a sixty-foot bar in here. It's got to be the main focal point of the place. Still to this day people come in and comment about the bar. It's big. It's usually twice the size of most places you go."

People also know immediately that Rocky River is a brewpub. To get to the steps, people must walk through a small breezeway that's smack in the middle of the brewing operation. On the left side—behind glass, of course—are the brew kettle and mash tun. On the right side are the fermenters.

Gary and brother Bob Cintron didn't know anything about the brewing industry before they started Rocky River in 1998. They had worked for years in the restaurant business when they got the chance to open their own place. While they were researching what type of place to open, they walked into a former brewpub in Cincinnati and fell in love.

"The stainless steel tanks. The manufacturing idea of it," Gary Cintron said. "At that point, we were right on the uprise of breweries in the coun-

Beers brewed: Year-round: Pirate Light, Cooper's Gold Kolsch, and Blueberry Ale. Rocky River typically has eight or nine house beers on tap, so there are plenty of rotating and seasonal selections.

The Pick: It's tough to pick one because there are so many rotating beers here. But try the Pirate Light, the brewpub's best-seller. It's remarkably tasty for a golden-colored American blonde ale with only 4.6 percent alcohol. It's what a lawnmower beer should taste like.

try. We came back here and pitched the idea [to the investors] and they loved it."

Good friend Charles Nagy, the former Cleveland Indians pitcher, is one of the investors and actually picked out the suburban location on Cleveland's west side. The brewpub is located along Center Ridge Road, a commercial and retail strip that includes the Westgate Mall. Since they didn't know anything about brewing, Gary Cintron went to a place that knew plenty for advice: Great Lakes Brewing Company. That's where Rocky River found its first brewer, Matt Cole, who now co-owns his own place on the west side of Cleveland, Fat Head's Brewery & Saloon.

Rocky River struck gold with Cole, who quickly earned a reputation as a creative brewer and put the brewpub on the map for discriminating beer drinkers. He racked up numerous medals at the Great American Beer Festival and World Beer Cup. Those medals now are framed and hang on one of the walls.

Jim Lieb, who worked for the now-closed Hereford & Hops in Pittsburgh, took over as brewer when Cole left and has continued to keep the quality and selection high. Rocky River usually has eight or nine house beers on tap, but only three regulars. And while most brewpubs might have a pale ale and amber among those regulars, Rocky River's standard beers are a light, a kolsch, and a blueberry ale. That means people often find new, rotating beers.

"For us, maybe it hurts, maybe it doesn't," Gary Cintron said. "But the thought is that when people come in they know we've got the standard beer and then it's a roll of the dice to see what else we have."

Lieb has great flexibility to brew whatever he wants. One of his most unusual creations was 65 Roses, a red ale brewed with rose hips that was made for a Cystic Fibrosis Foundation fundraiser. His goal, he said, is to brew a variety of beer that keeps people interested and coming back. As far as whether he leans toward hoppy or malty beers, Lieb rides the fence.

"My favorite beers are all over the place," he said.

Gary Cintron said one of the best pieces of advice he got early on from Great Lakes was not to try to bottle and distribute Rocky River beer. If Rocky River was going to be a brewpub, then be a brewpub. So many brewpubs have gone out of business because they tried to do that and the distribution side of the business dragged down the brewpub.

"My kids are always asking how come our beer isn't in the store. How come our beer is not here or there," Gary said. "The funny thing is from an ego point of view you'd love to have your beer at the store.

You'd love it. But not at the expense of losing what you have. We're happy and content with what we're doing. And we serve a purpose. We put out good products, food- and beer-wise, and in an industry where not everybody can say that."

Rocky River Brewing Company

Opened: 1998.

Owners: Gary Cintron and Bob Cintron.

Brewer: Jim Lieb.

System: 7-barrel Century system.

Production: 500 barrels.

Distribution: At the brewpub only.

Hours: The kitchen is open seven days a week from 11:30 A.M. to 11 P.M. There is a limited night menu from 11 P.M. to 1 A.M. The bar is open daily from 11:30 A.M. to 2 A.M.

Tours: Upon request.

Take-out beer: Growlers and kegs.

Food: The full menu features typical American fare, with appetizers, pizza, sandwiches, and entrees ranging from Pretzel Crusted Chicken to Eggplant Lasagna.

Parking: There is plenty of parking surrounding the brewpub.

Other area beer sites: See page 18.

The World Beer Tour

The Winking Lizard's World Beer Tour started simply enough in 1987. Customers would come into the original restaurant and bar in Bedford Heights in suburban Cleveland and drink forty different beers from around the world over the course of a calendar year. At the end of the so-called tour, anyone who accomplished the feat received a T-shirt with the names of the beers on it.

It was an ingenious promotion. The Winking Lizard wanted to move some different beers and give its clientele an incentive to return and spend money. And beer drinkers, who had limited choices in the Cleveland area in the late 1980s, wanted to try anything new and figured if they're going to drink beer they might as well get rewarded for it with a free prize. (When you think about it, the prize isn't really free since you're paying for a ton of beer—some of it quite pricey.)

Over the years, the World Beer Tour has grown in popularity, now boasting about six thousand participants annually. The Winking Lizard has expanded, as well, with restaurants throughout Northeast and Central Ohio. The chain is in Avon, Bedford Heights, Brunswick, Canton, Cleveland Heights, Cleveland, Columbus, Fairlawn, Independence, Lakewood, Macedonia, Mentor, and Peninsula.

The Winking Lizard also has developed into one of the best beer bars in the United States, offering hundreds of draft, bottled, and canned beer. Each restaurant, which serves typical brewpub fare such as burgers and salads, is set up like a sports bar with a large bar and plenty of dining area. There also are a lot of televisions and some videogames. Each location features a live lizard in a giant glass-enclosed cage—a popular spot for kids to press up against the glass and gawk at the reptile.

But back to the World Beer Tour. Here's how it works: You plunk down $10 to participate and receive a spiral-bound booklet that details all the beers available, a little cheat sheet that allows you to cross off the beers you've had, and a card that looks like a credit card that keeps track of all the beers you've drank.

It's not as simple as it once was to polish off the tour. Today, people have to finish one hundred beers in a year instead of forty. Finish fifty and you'll get a halfway prize, which often is a T-shirt. Hit the century mark and you'll get a better prize, which has ranged from quality fleece jackets to a down winter vest sporting the Winking Lizard logo. With an eye toward charity, the Winking Lizard also has started giving people the option of not collecting their jacket at the end of the tour and instead donating $50 to the Coats for Kids program.

For the record, one person doesn't have to drink all one hundred beers alone. For example, husbands and wives can work together on the same tour. But sorry, there's only one prize awarded for each tour.

There's also nothing stopping anyone from doing the tour more than once in a single year. The record is seventeen times. Yes, that is 1,700 beers in a year or nearly five beers a day. The Winking Lizard doesn't endorse or recommend doing the tour that many times. Neither does its insurance carrier.

At the outset, the tour was pretty rigid. People had to finish preselected bottled beers, meaning if you knew you didn't like a certain brand, you had to choke it down anyway—or have a friend drink it—to claim your prize. But that also has changed over time. The tour now features more than 240 choices in bottles, cans, and on draft, so people can skip a beer they know they won't enjoy.

The tour features a healthy mix of American craft brewers and selections from around the world. Each year, the beers change, although there are some holdovers and many of the breweries represented stay the same. For example, Stone, Sierra Nevada, Samuel Smith, Orval, Brooklyn, Lindemans, and Ayinger all make annual appearances.

John Lane, who runs the World Beer Tour and has been with the chain for more than two decades, admits that the tour is light-years ahead of where it started. In the beginning, the organizers focused more on picking the prize than the beers.

"We didn't know a whole hell of a lot about beer back then," he said. "Everybody would get in a room and literally taste 150 beers at the same time and we'd say, 'Yeah, I like this.' 'No, I don't like that.'"

The original tour featured beers like Negro Modelo, Guinness, and Samuel Smith. Those are household brands today, but were considered rare finds in an area dominated by national brands and still untouched by the craft beer movement in the late 1980s.

A few years into the tour, Lane picked up a book by renowned beer guide and author Michael Jackson and started learning more about the craft. A sales representative from specialty beer importer Merchant du Vin also started teaching him about beer.

"That's when I came up with a brainstorm that if we're really going to do this thing, we're going to have to educate our customers," Lane said. "If we could educate the consumer, we're going to have a buying consumer."

He created a crude, black-and-white guidebook that provided a description of each beer. That turned into a color, spiral-bound booklet over the years.

Lane's job selecting the beers has gotten harder in recent years, because the quality of beer and choices available have improved. It's also more difficult to manage a tour with six thousand people. (He estimates that only thirty-five hundred people finish the tour each year.) Despite the enormous amount of American craft beer available, Lane, who estimated that he samples anywhere from seven hundred to one thousand beers a year, will always have beers from around the world such as Orval and Ayinger represented on the tour.

"While the craft movement is such a . . . wonderful thing, I also believe you have to go back to your roots as well and understand where that culture came from," he said. "It's from the old countries. It's from the Czech Republic. It's from Germany. It's from Belgium. It's from England. We might not be doing what we're doing without those old countries."

Lane's personal favorites include Orval, Hoegaarden, Great Lakes Edmund Fitzgerald, and Sierra Nevada Pale Ale.

As the World Beer Tour celebrated its twenty-fifth anniversary in 2011, Lane admitted he's astonished at its popularity now. "It's almost surreal. Come on, six thousand people?"

For more details about the tour and how to participate, go online to www.winkinglizard.com.

Northeast Ohio

Ohioans are likely wondering why Cleveland isn't included in this chapter on Northeast Ohio. Cleveland is Northeast Ohio to many people. But there are just so many breweries in Cleveland and its immediate suburbs, and still more scattered just beyond, that a combined single chapter would be too unwieldy.

On top of that, there are plenty of large communities outside of Cleveland with their own identities and economies. Take Akron, for example. It has a metropolitan population of about seven hundred thousand. Not exactly a tiny town, but Akron is often overshadowed by neighboring Cleveland, which is only about forty miles to the north. Then there's Youngstown, Canton, Massillon, Warren, and Ashtabula.

Akron's claim to fame—before LeBron James, that is—was the rubber industry. The rubber factories have long disappeared but the city is still home to the worldwide headquarters of Goodyear Tire & Rubber Company. And with that distinction comes blimps. It's not unusual to see one of the famous Goodyear blimps slowly floating by on any given day.

Lockheed Martin still builds military airships at the massive Goodyear Airdock, which was constructed in 1929 as a place to build the blimps. The building, which is not open to the public, is more than 364,000 square feet. It is listed in the National Register of Historic Places.

The Akron area is big on higher education. The University of Akron, which has about twenty-six thousand students, is located in the city. And just down the road in nearby Kent is Kent State University, the second-largest public university in Ohio with more than forty thousand students on its multiple campuses. Akron has three production breweries: Thirsty Dog Brewing Company, Hoppin' Frog Brewery, and Ohio Brewing Company. All have started up since 2005.

Youngstown is the next-largest city in the region. The community is known for steel mills and working-class folk. It's home to Youngstown State University, which has more than fourteen thousand students, and the Butler Institute of Art, a museum dedicated to American art.

Here's a look at some beer-related options.

- **The Winking Lizard restaurants** (www.winkinglizard.com) have already been mentioned in the Cleveland chapter as a great place to get a beer. Well, there are plenty of them located outside of the immediate Cleveland area as well.

- **69 Taps** (www.69taps.com), which has bars in Akron, Medina, and Wadsworth, is another great place to have a beer. As you might guess, the bars feature an extensive list of draft beers with plenty of American craft and imports. And yes, there are sixty-nine taps.

- **Ray's Place** (135 Franklin Avenue, Kent, 330-673-2233, www .raysplacekent.com) has been an institution in the college town since 1937. The bar—where former Kent State students Drew Carey and Joe Walsh were known to hang out—has sixty taps and more than 125 bottled beers. The hole-in-the-wall underwent a major renovation in 2007.

- **Vintage Estate Wine and Beer** (7317 South Avenue, Boardman, 330-629-8080, www.vewinebeer.com) is the place to go for take-out beer. It was rated the best beer retailer in the world in 2010 by Ratebeer.com. The store features more than eight hundred craft beers and more than one thousand wines.

Here are other interesting places to visit while traveling through Northeast Ohio.

- **Wine Trails** (www.ohiowines.org). Northeast Ohio—and Ashtabula and Lake Counties, in particular—is home to many wineries. You'll find the state's only estate winery and brewery, Debonne Vineyards and Cellar Rats Brewery, in Madison. If you're interested in a wine tour while you're visiting area breweries, check out the Ohio Wine Producers Association website. There's a full listing of wine trails in the state.

- **Cuyahoga Valley National Park** (800-257-9477, www.nps.gov/cuva) is Ohio's only national park. Covering 33,000 acres and located between Akron and Cleveland, the park includes forests, rolling hills, and farmland. The park follows the winding Cuyahoga River.

And while in the park, you may want to take a ride on the **Cuyahoga Valley Scenic Railroad** (2325 Stine Road, Peninsula, 800-468-4070, www.cvsr.com). The railroad offers rides all year round from various stations.

- **The Pro Football Hall of Fame** (2121 George Halas Drive NW, Canton, 330-456-8207, www.profootballhof.com) is a must-visit for any pro football fan. It's where all of the NFL greats are enshrined. The community puts on a huge ten-day festival every year at the end of July and beginning of August for the enshrinement ceremony and Hall of Fame Game, which kicks off the NFL preseason.

- **Paul Brown Tiger Stadium** (www.massillonproud.com) is also a must for football fans. Sure, it's just a high school field, but folks in Massillon take their football seriously—very seriously. Paul Brown, who went on to coach the Ohio State University Buckeyes, Cleveland Browns, and Cincinnati Bengals, once coached the Massillon team. Every baby boy born in the community is given a miniature football and the team mascot is a live tiger cub named Obie. The community's passion was featured in the 2001 documentary *Go Tigers!*

- **The National First Ladies' Library** (205 Market Avenue S., Canton, 330-452-0876, www.firstladies.org) may seem an odd suggestion for a beer travel book, but there *is* the famous story of first lady and Ohioan Florence Harding, wife of President Warren G. Harding, allowing alcohol to be served in the White House during Prohibition.

- **Harry London Candies** (5353 Lauby Road, North Canton, 800-321-0444, ext. 119, www.harrylondon.com) has made chocolate candies here since 1922. The company offers tours, but you need an advance reservation. Its store sells more than five hundred varieties of candy.

Cellar Rats Brewery

7743 Doty Road, Madison, OH 44057
(440) 466-3485 • www.ratbrew.com

Tony Debevc Jr. saw it all the time. People would visit the family-owned Debonne Vineyards, but not everyone would taste the wine. Some folks just don't like wine.

So Debevc, vice president of operations for the winery, and Ed Trebets, a chemist-winemaker at Debonne, decided to open a brewery there in May 2008, creating Ohio's only estate winery and brewery and one of the few such operations in the United States.

Cellar Rats Brewery operates as a separate business, but is located on the property, and beer tastings are given the same treatment as wine tastings.

"We wanted to target a whole new audience," Debevc said. "We had a lot of people who used to come here—between men and women—who'd always say, 'Aww, my husband doesn't drink wine. Aww, my girlfriend doesn't drink wine. She's a beer drinker.' That was another driving factor of why we wanted to get into this. And the main thing is me and Ed love beer."

He estimated that the addition of the brewery, which offers its beer on draft and in bottles, has boosted tourism by 10 percent.

"We're affiliated with the winery," Debevc said. "And we're not trying to hide that we're on our own. The winery has brought most of our customer base to us. Now that the brewery is building its own, we're also bringing customers to the winery."

Anton Debevc founded the vineyard in 1916, and in 1971, the Debevc family established Chalet Debonne Vineyards in Madison. It's now Ohio's largest estate winery, producing about 34,000 cases of wine a year. The winery is located in Northeast Ohio's Grand River Valley just south of Lake Erie and Interstate 90. The region includes five wineries that banded together to create the Winegrowers of the Grand River Valley.

Cellar Rats and Debonne are set on a sprawling estate with 127 acres of grapes. The main building

Beers brewed: Year-round: Pack Rat Pilsner, Field Rat Wheat Beer, Rat Tail Ale, InFESTation, Black Rat Imperial Stout, Rampage IPA, and Ratsberry Plague Porter. There also are rotating and seasonal beers.

The Pick: The Ratsberry Plague Porter is a creamy espresso-laced porter with natural raspberry flavoring. It's a tasty dark fruit beer.

is set up as a chalet, with plenty of space for visitors, including regular bus tours. There's a wine-tasting room, beer-tasting room, gift shop, outdoor picnic tables, and large patio where live music and cookouts are held on Fridays, Saturdays, and Sundays during the summer.

As with all wineries, Debonne, and now Cellar Rats, thrives on drop-in visitors and bus tours hauling wine enthusiasts from one winery to another. Some are shocked, pleasantly of course, to find a brewery at the location. Debevc said some people have cut their bus tours short after discovering the brewery, opting to remain at Debonne and Cellar Rats instead of continuing on.

Debevc used to brew on a small, three-barrel system and admitted that it was hard sometimes to keep up with demand, especially since he works for both the winery and brewery. It's really difficult at grape harvest time. The fact that he likes to have more than ten Cellar Rats beers on tap doesn't make it any easier. Keeping up with demand became a little easier in 2011. The company constructed a new building and bought a new 15-barrel system and bottling line. Up until that point, the beer had been available only on draft.

So what's up with the Cellar Rats name? Rats don't have the best reputation when it comes to cleanliness, but the name stems from the winery term for a cellar worker instead of the actual rodent.

"The term 'cellar rat' has been in the wine industry for decades," Debevc said. "It was a guy in the cellar with no windows, wet, dirty, grungy. He was always downstairs. He was always in the dark. He was always wet. Just like a rat in a sewer."

All the Cellar Rats beers have some "rat" in their name, including Rat Trap Lager, Pack Rat Pilsner, Field Rat Wheat Beer, and Ratsberry Plague Porter. Even a name that doesn't scream "rat" like Karni Mata IPA has some rat reference; Karni Mata is the goddess of rats in India.

When it comes to the beer itself, Debevc said he's not interested in brewing to beer-style guidelines so he can win beer competitions. He said he often hears people say they like the beer, but it doesn't fit to a style that would take home a medal at the Great American Beer Festival. He makes no apologies for that.

"I'm glad we're selling beer," he said. "When I do a recipe, I'm not going for style. I'm going for our style so people say, 'God I like that beer. It's different from what I had in New York. It's different from what I had in Michigan.' It's not a standard lager. It's not a standard porter. That's our direction. We're doing what we want and what makes us happy. And our customers like it, too."

Cellar Rats Brewery

Opened: 2008.

Owners: Tony Debevc Jr. and Ed Trebets.

Brewer: Tony Debevc Jr.

System: 15-barrel Premier Stainless system.

Production: 280 barrels.

Distribution: At the brewery and restaurants, bars, and stores in northeast Ohio.

Hours: Monday and Tuesday, noon to 6 P.M.; Wednesday and Friday, noon to 11 P.M.; Thursday and Saturday, noon to 8 P.M.; and Sunday, 1 P.M. to 6 P.M. In January, hours are Monday through Saturday, noon to 6 P.M.

Tours: Monday through Saturday after 2 P.M.

Take-out beer: Growlers and bottles.

Extras: Cellar Rats is located at the Debonne Vineyard, so there is plenty of wine to taste in addition to beer. There's also live music and cookouts on Fridays, Saturdays, and Sundays during the summer.

Parking: A large lot is out front.

Other area beer sites: See page 54.

Chardon BrewWorks & Eatery

205 Main Street, Chardon, OH 44024
440-286-9001 • www.chardonbrewworks.com

Chardon BrewWorks & Eatery can be found in rural Geauga County, a community located about thirty miles east of downtown Cleveland. The county is well-known mainly for two things: Amish and maple syrup. Both are major tourist attractions.

The county is home to about fourteen thousand Amish, making it one of the largest Amish settlements in the world. There are plenty of Amish craft stores, bakeries, and kitchens dotting the community, not to mention antiques shops.

Then there's the maple syrup industry. The folks here take their syrup seriously. Each March, there is a special tapping ceremony when a hole is drilled into a maple tree and sap comes oozing out. The community also holds the annual Geauga County Maple Festival, a four-day event in April on Chardon Square in downtown Chardon, a town of about five thousand people and the county seat. As you might guess, it's a celebration of maple syrup.

Oh, and there's one more thing that Chardon and Geauga County are known for—snow. The community is in the so-called "snow belt" and gets hammered in the winter, so be forewarned if you take a trip. Chardon doesn't hide from its snowy reputation. The city even has a link on its website where people can check historic snowfall totals. The average is more than 107 inches a season.

Chardon Square is a large rectangular greenspace that features a historic white bandstand built in 1875. The square is surrounded by small retail shops and other businesses, and one of those happens to be Chardon BrewWorks.

Mike and Donna Nedrow opened the brewpub in 2010 after years of homebrewing. The first batch Mike made was a hefeweizen named Donna Do Ya Wanna. It's now available at the brewpub.

The brewpub sits in an attractive row building, the kind you would find in any picturesque little historic American downtown. It doesn't have a typical brewpub feel. Why's that? Well, there are two main things missing when you walk in. You'll be hard-pressed to see the bar, and there's no brewing equipment in sight. Instead, the atmosphere is more about dining. The bar is in the back of the restaurant and up a flight of steps. It's a small, cozy area.

The brewhouse is not in the restaurant area. Instead, it's accessible through another door in the front of the building and up a flight of steps.

Beers brewed: Kolonel Klink Kolsch, Courthouse Porter, Ironworker IPA, Donna Do Ya Wanna Hefeweizen, Matzenweizen, and Working Man Pale Ale were on tap when I visited.

The Pick: The Donna Do Ya Wanna Hefeweizen is a solid unfiltered wheat served with a lemon slice. The beer has a decent clove and banana aroma and flavor.

Chardon BrewWorks & Eatery

Opened: 2010.

Owner: Mike and Donna Nedrow.

System: Brew Magic system.

Distribution: At the brewpub only.

Hours: Tuesday, Wednesday, and Thursday, 11:30 A.M. to 9 P.M.; and Friday and Saturday, 11:30 A.M. to 11 P.M.

Tours: None available.

Food: Chardon BrewWorks offers typical brewpub fare ranging from quesadillas to burgers. Entrées also include 12-ounce strip steak, pasta, and apple bourbon chicken.

Extras: Occasional entertainment, including karaoke and bands.

Parking: There is on-street parking out front.

Other area beer sites: See page 54.

Chardon BrewWorks & Eatery   **59**

Hoppin' Frog Brewery

1680-F E. Waterloo Road, Akron, OH 44306
330-352-4578 • www.hoppinfrog.com

Hoppin' Frog Brewery owner and brewer Fred Karm has no problem celebrating being seventeeth, as in the seventeenth-best brewery in the world. At least that's where Ratebeer.com ranked his small operation on the south side of Akron in 2011. Karm is so proud of that honor that he slapped it onto a T-shirt for sale at the brewery.

It's quite an achievement for a guy who once thought brewing was too much effort. In 1994, a friend asked Karm to help him brew a batch of beer. He had a good time but was turned off by how long it took and how much labor was involved. He told his friend that he never wanted to help him again.

A month later, his friend invited him to a homebrew club meeting. The pair won a pound of barley and an ounce of hops. His friend insisted that Karm take it and make some beer. After some initial misgivings, Karm started making beer with friends and hasn't stopped since. He and his friends became so obsessed that first year that he estimated they brewed almost every weekend and made fifty batches.

Karm later won a medal at a homebrew contest and was asked in late 1996 to join the Thirsty Dog Brewing Company as the brewer. At the time, Thirsty Dog was opening a chain of brewpubs. Karm, who left a job as an electrical engineer, continued his success as a professional brewer and racked up numerous medals at the Great American Beer Festival for his Thirsty Dog recipes.

But when the Thirsty Dog brewpubs closed down, he was out of a job. He decided to open his own brewpub, but was unable to secure enough financing on his own to start a restaurant. Instead, he opted to open a production brewery in 2006.

The operation is in a small industrial park along the busy U.S. Route 224 and not far from Interstate 77. The building itself is a nondescript concrete block facility. It's located across the

Beers brewed: Year-round: B.O.R.I.S. the Crusher Oatmeal-Imperial Stout, Barrel Aged B.O.R.I.S. Oatmeal-Imperial Stout, Outta Kilter Wee-Heavy Scotch Red Ale, Mean Manalishi Double IPA, Silk Porter, and Hoppin' to Heaven IPA. Hoppin' Frog also makes ten seasonal beers.

The Pick: The Barrel Aged B.O.R.I.S. Oatmeal-Imperial Stout is outstanding. It pours and looks like motor oil, with slight carbonation. The flavor is complex with bourbon, vanilla, wood, and roasted malts all coming through.

street from the gigantic Goodyear Airdock, where Goodyear would build and house its famous blimps that seem to fly over every sporting event imaginable. Lockheed Martin now uses the airdock to build airships for the military. With Goodyear Tire & Rubber Company based in Akron, it's not unusual at all to see the famous Goodyear blimps hovering above the community.

Karm named his brewery Hoppin' Frog for a reason. His nickname is "Frog." Why? Well, his dad's name also is Fred and the family needed to call him something different. Somewhere along the way it became "Frog" and it just stuck. Karm also liked the use of "Hoppin'," which describes the atmosphere at the small brewery and is a play on the essential beer ingredient.

The logo is a frog standing up and holding a mug of beer. A giant version of the logo is painted on one of the yellow walls inside the brewery. Hoppin' Frog isn't a big operation. There's nothing separating visitors from the brewhouse or the small production area, so when people walk through the front door, they walk into the actual brewery. Sometimes, customers will visit as a small crew of volunteers is bottling the unfiltered beers by hand.

At the front of the brewery is a small cooler for retail sales. Hoppin' Frog also sells T-shirts, hats, and other clothing with its logo.

Karm has earned a well-deserved reputation and a loyal following for making flavorful, high-alcohol beers. His slogan is "We make flavorful beers in the most flavorful styles." Most of his brews clock in at more than 7 percent alcohol, and with the beer being sold in 22-ounce bottles that's quite a punch.

He has continued to win medals at the Great American Beer Festival and his beers consistently receive rave reviews from critics on BeerAdvocate.com and Ratebeer.com. His B.O.R.I.S. the Crusher Oatmeal-Imperial Stout and the Barrel Aged B.O.R.I.S. Oatmeal-Imperial Stout have shown up on Ratebeer.com's annual lists of the best one hundred beers in the world.

"It's a thrill beyond belief," Karm said about all the accolades. "I'm very, very, very lucky . . . it's really amazing what we've achieved for a small brewery in such a short time."

He has a simple philosophy when it comes to making beer. He wants to brew beers that he, his friends, and his family like. It just so happens that the public enjoys them, too.

"I'm brewing these for me," Karm said. "That's what I'm most proud of, I think, because I've been able to market these beers that I absolutely love. And I spare no expense in brewing these. I buy the [stuff] I want to brew. I buy the [stuff] I want to brew with. I'm just very, very lucky to be able to make these killer beers to satisfy me and everybody else likes them, too. It couldn't be any better."

Hoppin' Frog Brewery

Opened: 2006.
Owner: Fred Karm.
Brewer: Fred Karm.
System: 10-barrel JV Northwest system.
Production: 800 barrels.
Distribution: Ohio, Florida, Georgia, Indiana, Illinois, Kansas, Massachusetts, New Jersey, New York, North Carolina, Pennsylvania, Rhode Island, South Carolina and Virginia, along with Denmark, Italy, Netherlands, Norway, Sweden, and Switzerland.
Hours: Call ahead. Karm is there almost every afternoon, but there are no regular hours.
Tours: By appointment only.
Take-out beer: 22-ounce bottles.
Parking: There is a parking lot outside the business.
Other area beer sites: See page 54.

Lager Heads Smokehouse & Brewery

2832 Abbeyville Road, Medina, OH 44256
330-725-1947 • www.lagerheads.us

The name Lager Heads screams brewery. Or at least beer. But Lager Heads Smokehouse & Brewery didn't start out as a brewery at all. It was just a popular barbecue restaurant off the beaten path in northern Medina County back when it opened in 2004.

Brothers Matt and Jon Kiene were looking for a new career challenge and had been talking about opening a restaurant for years. At the time, Matt was in sales and Jon was working in construction.

They heard about this little bar up for sale in Abbeyville, an unincorporated area just north of the city of Medina. The Kienes had grown up a mile from the bar and figured it would be a great location for their restaurant.

"Quite honestly this building was a disaster when we bought it so it was priced right and something we could afford even though we had to dump a ton of money and work into it that we did ourselves," Matt Kiene said.

The work shows. The restaurant is casual dining with a rustic feel. There are wooden floors, exposed wooden beams, two boar heads and turtle shells hanging in the bar area, and a historical Abbeyville sign on the wall. There are also framed posters of renegades on one wall—Clint Eastwood from one of his westerns, Dennis Hopper and Peter Fonda from *Easy Rider*, Paul Newman and Robert Redford from *Butch Cassidy and the Sundance Kid*, and reggae superstar Bob Marley, who seems a tad out of place next to the others.

"It's not stuffy here," Jon Kiene said. "It's comfortable. It's a relaxed fun place."

Early on, Lager Heads earned a solid reputation for barbecue, especially because it smokes its own meats and there wasn't another barbecue joint like it in the county. The menu ranges from pulled pork sandwiches to St. Louis–style ribs to smoked chicken wings.

"Everything revolves around our hickory smoker as far as the restaurant goes," Matt Kiene said. "Everything we do here for the most part is homemade from scratch, from our sauces to, obviously, the beer, and from the way we cook our meats up to twelve to fourteen hours. I hope you're not in a hurry when you come out here. We take time to do it right. And everything is as authentic as we can make it."

As the restaurant gained popularity, the brothers thought that brewing their own beer would be a great marriage with the barbecue. The Kienes are both homebrewers and big beer fans. They made sure the restaurant was stocked with a large assortment of craft beer—up to sixty brands at one time. And the craft beer sold well.

"It just seemed like the perfect fit for the restaurant," Matt Kiene said.

Oddly enough, old maps from the 1880s indicate there was a brewery just a hundred yards away from the Lager Heads site. It's unclear what the name was, though.

It took a little while for the brewery to get off the ground thanks to the financial crisis and banks tightening up on lending money, but the Lager Heads Brewing Company eventually debuted in June 2010. The Kienes hired Steve Bagley as the head brewer. Bagley was no stranger

Beers brewed: Year-round: Tyranny Pale Ale, Bed Head Red, Savage Stout, and Barnburner Lager. The brewery also makes seasonals and rotating beers.

The Pick: Try the Abbeyville Abbey. The strong Belgian ale is served in a snifter glass and is 10 percent alcohol. But be careful: The beer is deceptively smooth and doesn't overwhelm with a big alcohol flavor.

to Lager Heads. He had visited the restaurant years earlier and inquired whether it was a brewpub given its name. Go figure that he would later become the brewer.

In another comical twist, Bagley has a full-time job at an area wastewater treatment plant. So essentially, the brewery operation keeps him in business at the plant.

"All the beers that we make are bold without being over the top," said Matt Kiene, who's partial to Belgian beers. "Our goal is to put out bold beers that are easy on the palate and can be enjoyed by the masses."

The Kienes have big goals for the brewing side of the business. They'd like to become a regional brewer and in 2011 started bottling their beer. For now, they just hope people keep seeking out Lager Heads.

"We're a destination spot," Matt Kiene said. "We're off the beaten path. You've got to want to come out here."

Lager Heads Smokehouse & Brewery

Opened: 2010 (the restaurant opened in 2004).

Owners: Matt and Jon Kiene.

Brewers: Steve Bagley and Brian Caton.

System: 15-barrel system.

Production: 1,000 barrels.

Distribution: At Lager Heads and on draft and in bottles at various bars and restaurants throughout Medina, Summit, Lake, and Cuyahoga Counties.

Hours: Monday through Thursday, 11 A.M. to 11 P.M.; Friday and Saturday, 11 A.M. to 1 A.M.; and Sunday, 11 A.M. to 10 P.M.

Tours: Available upon request.

Take-out beer: Growlers.

Food: The menu features all kinds of barbecue, from smoked chicken wings to beef brisket.

Parking: There is parking around the building, but it can be crowded during dinner time.

Other area beer sites: See page 54.

Little Mountain Brewing Company

9374 Chillicothe Road, Kirtland, OH 44094
440-256-1645 • www.littlemountainbrewing.com

Bob Weber had always thought about opening his own brewery. The longtime homebrewer figured it would be great to turn his passion into a career, but like a lot of folks, he was worried about the risk. Then, the economy tumbled and he lost his job in the heating and air-conditioning industry. He searched for work for months but couldn't find anything.

"I finally looked at my wife and I said, 'You know what? We have to do something. We can't sit here and wait for the phone to ring. If there's ever going to be a time when I do this, it's going to be now. So let's try it,'" he said. "[The economy] pushed me into it. I probably wouldn't have ever taken the risk. It turned from being a risk to almost being a necessity."

Weber is enjoying the risk-necessity so far. He opened Little Mountain Brewing Company, a brew-on-premises business and brewery in 2010. The brewery shares a small strip mall in Kirtland with a convenience store, hair salon, and bar. Kirtland is a far-flung eastern suburb of Cleveland, just south of Interstate 90 and Lake Erie. The community has about seven thousand people.

The Little Mountain name comes from a Lake County landmark. Little Mountain is the highest point in the county at 1,227 feet. Plenty of businesses use the name, including the Little Mountain Country Club and Little Mountain Homebrewers Association.

"We wanted something that was a little bit natural, earthy to go with our beer, and we wanted something to identify us with Lake County, so Little Mountain met both of those criteria," Weber said.

The focus is the brew-on-premises operation, which allows people to make an appointment and brew any style of beer they want under the guidance of a professional brewer. Little Mountain supplies the equipment, recipes, and ingredients and even cleans up after you. The customer supplies

Beers brewed: Little Mountain plans to offer at least six rotating house beers. During my visit, the menu included Belgian Wit, Saint Graal, Lakeshore Lager, Mad Hornet, Irish Red, and Hells Bells.

The Pick: Saint Graal is a Belgian tripel with nine percent alcohol. It has a powerful alcohol mouth feel.

the elbow grease and the fun. The brewing process is seen as a social event and groups of people often will brew together.

The brew-on-premises phenomenon started in Canada in the early 1980s because beer taxes were so high there. It later migrated to the United States and has been received with mixed popularity here. In Northeast Ohio, The Brew Kettle (see page 23) operates an immensely popular brew-on-premises business, but others, such as the Brew Keeper and Beer Factory, have failed to last.

Weber wanted to fill the void on Cleveland's east side and also figured the brew-on-premises business was a way for him to start making his own beer on a commercial basis. Little Mountain is making both draft and bottled beer, and it's available for sampling at the small brewery. He also planned to have it available at some select bars and restaurants in the Kirtland area.

Weber took great pains in transforming the interior of the storefront business, which at 1,200 square feet isn't very big at all. He wanted to create an English pub feel and give the brewery a more upscale look than just a spot to manufacture beer. There is a small bar with a ceramic-tile top, wooden floors, brick paneling, and what at first appears to be a tin ceiling that's really just well-designed plastic panels.

"It's just a good place to stop and talk beer and meet with your peers," Weber said when asked to describe the brewery.

He really enjoys the camaraderie that comes along with brew-on-premises operations. There are always interesting people to chat with who are interested in beer.

Weber has six house beers available that rotate depending on the season and what he is most interested in at the time. Weber enjoys wheat and Belgian beers, and people can expect those styles to be well represented. One of his goals, he said, is to brew many different styles and offer some beers that people normally don't get to taste.

"I like to see the happy look on other people's faces when they drink our beers," he said. "It's one of the great joys in life."

Little Mountain Brewing Company

Opened: 2010.
Owner: Bob Weber.
Brewer: Bob Weber.
System: Six 15-gallon Custom Brew Beer systems.

Production: 200 to 300 barrels.

Distribution: At the brewery and some bars and restaurants in the Kirtland area.

Hours: Wednesday through Friday, 5 P.M. to 10 P.M.; Saturday, 10 A.M. to 6 P.M.; and Sunday, noon to 6 P.M. Other times are available by appointment to brew.

Take-out beer: Bottles, growlers, and some smaller kegs are available.

Tours: None.

Food: A bar-restaurant in the same strip mall provides food for the brewery.

Parking: There is a large lot out front.

Other area beer sites: See page 54.

Main Street Grille & Brewing Company

8148 Main Street, Garrettsville, OH 44231
330-527-3663 • www.msg-brew.com

For many Garrettsville residents, the Main Street Grille & Brewing Company will always be known as "The Mill." The historic, wooden building dates back to 1804, and as the nickname implies, it once housed a flour mill.

Built by village patriarch Col. John Garrett, the mill sits along Main Street and the back of the brewpub hangs over Silver Creek, a gorge, a small waterfall, and a water wheel that can still power a working mill in the basement.

"We could still grind flour if I wanted to. We are fully operational. The wheel spins. The grinder works. And as times get worse, we might go back to grinding flour," owner Pete Kepich said, laughing.

Kepich, who owns a Ford car dealership in town, and his wife, Peggy, didn't know anything about brewing when they bought the vacant building and opened the brewpub in 2007. It had sat empty for a few years after a previous brewpub failed. They were more interested in the restaurant side of the

Beers brewed: Year-round: Garrett's Gold, River Rat Amber, Edelweizen, and '35 Extra Stout. There also are many rotating and seasonal beers.

The Pick: The Progress Porter is so unusual you have to try it. It's a mild porter aged on crushed Arabica espresso beans. There's a huge coffee aroma and flavor, almost like drinking a carbonated espresso.

business, because there aren't many places to get a good meal in Garrettsville, a rural village of about twenty-three hundred people in northeastern Ohio. They also wanted to see a landmark building reopen in their town.

The brewpub is in a beautiful setting downtown. The building itself resembles a general store from the Old West, with its wooden frame and front porch. There's a patio and walkway in the back of the restaurant that overlook the creek. The interior is stunning, with worn wooden floors, exposed wooden beams, and a two-story ceiling in the bar area. The backsplash of the bar is composed of large rocks taken from the creek outside.

The dining area overlooks the waterfall. There are framed black-and-white photos of the mill on the wall, including one photo of the building engulfed in flames. The small copper brewhouse sits on a loft built above the bar and customers can gaze upward and see the brewing equipment.

There's something else interesting about the place. A young girl who died there years ago supposedly haunts the brewpub. People have reported seeing the girl standing in the front window or on the porch. Pete and Peggy Kepich have encountered strange instances when tables were moved and nobody was in the building.

"I've never seen it. I've never seen a ghost in here," Pete Kepich said. "I've heard weird things there's no doubt about it. But they're friendly. And they like our beer. That's why they're not bothering us."

It was a struggle to get the small brewery going. The equipment had sat unused for several years and needed a major overhaul. The brewpub didn't start making beer until a year after opening.

"I don't know how to relate it," Kepich said. "I'm in the car business, so it was like when we got in here the engine was blown, the tranny was scattered and the rear end wasn't even on the car."

Brewer Virgil Drayer-Reed, who was a homebrewer before being hired at Main Street, worked out the kinks and is now producing four regular beers and a slew of rotating and seasonal beers. The restaurant has an eclectic menu ranging from regular bar food, like hamburgers, to more upscale offerings, like lobster and filet mignon.

The brewery industry is nothing like the car business, where dealerships compete heavily for customers in a cutthroat way. Kepich was shocked that brewers are so helpful with each other.

"It's almost as if we could pick up the phone and have anybody from any brewery help us," he said. "That's amazing. What other business can you do that in? I've never seen a business so eager to see people prosper . . . I find that refreshing in the business world because you don't see that."

Despite being near Interstates 80 and 76, Main Street is off the beaten path. It's nearly a half-hour drive from Warren and longer from Youngstown—the two closest large cities. But craft beer drinkers have found the brewpub, nonetheless. Kepich estimated that people from twenty different states and Canada have stopped by to sample the beer.

"We want to have everybody walk out of here wowed. And that's our goal," he said.

Main Street Grille & Brewing Company

Opened: 2007.

Owners: Pete and Peggy Kepich.

Brewer: Virgil Drayer-Reed.

System: 3$1/2$-barrel DME Brewing Services.

Production: 100 barrels.

Distribution: At the brewpub and at Arabica coffeehouse in Streetsboro.

Hours: Tuesday, Wednesday, and Thursday, 11:30 A.M. to 9 P.M.; Friday and Saturday, 11 A.M. to 2 A.M.; Sunday, noon to 8 P.M. Closed on Monday.

Tours: Upon request.

Take-out beer: Growlers.

Food: An eclectic menu that includes salmon, filet mignon, pasta, and hamburgers. The menu also changes each season.

Extras: The brewpub holds the Frozen Falls Beer Festival in late January. It features craft beer from Ohio and western Pennsylvania.

Parking: There is on-street parking around the restaurant.

Other area beer sites: See page 54.

Ohio Brewing Company

451 S. High Street, Suite B, Akron, OH 44311
330-252-8004 • www.ohiobrewing.com

Ohio Brewing has been through a lot over the years. Owners Chris and Michael Verich started it as a brewpub in Niles in 1997. That location fizzled. They reopened in downtown Akron in 2008 under a partnership with Damon's Grill. Unfortunately, they opened the second brewpub during a recession and that location—on the first floor of the former O'Neil's department store—also struggled.

The Veriches, though, haven't wanted to give up on their brewing dreams. The company was reformed in 2010 and opened again as Chris's Akron Brewing Company. The brewery makes the same lineup of beers as in the past and still uses the Ohio Brewing name, but there is a major difference this time: There's no brewpub. Ohio Brewing is now strictly a production brewery.

The beer side of the business has always been the most successful, and Chris Verich said he wanted to focus on making beer, as opposed to worrying about operating a restaurant.

"This is what we always really wanted to do," said Chris Verich, vice president of the Ohio Craft Brewers Association and a former state representative. "I've gone through so many different versions of the brewery that I must love it if I'm still here. A lot of people would have given up, especially with Ohio being a tough market. But I believed in our products. I believe in the name Ohio Brewing. We've had a lot of fans who have stuck by us for years."

The new production brewery is located in the historic Selle Generator Works building, a small brick industrial complex that's been turned into a business incubator in downtown Akron. The building is about a mile south of the heart of downtown and near where the brewpub used to be. The brewery isn't open to the general public, but the hope in the future is to open a taproom where people can come and sample the beer.

Beers brewed: Year-round: Verich Gold, Cardinal Ale, O'Hoppy Ale, Alt-ernative Amber, and Steel Valley Stout. The brewery also makes seasonal beers.

The Pick: The Verich Gold won the People's Choice award at the 2010 Cleveland Labor Day Oktoberfest. A dry and clean-tasting kolsch, it's the lightest beer in the Ohio lineup.

Ohio Brewing—with its slogan "Brewers of Award Winning Beers"—is making both draft and bottled beer.

After years of having Ohio Brewing beer available only on draft, Chris Verich loves seeing it in bottles again. (The brewery briefly bottled when it was in Niles.)

"I really love seeing it in bottles where I can go to a grocery store or beer-wine store and see it up there. It's almost like you're a real brewery now," he said. "Now we've fully hit the market and people can enjoy our products in the comfort of their home. It's really starting to help our draft sales, too."

Chris is an avid traveler who makes sure he stops by breweries whenever he's in a new town. He estimated that he's visited more than six hundred breweries around the world. That's how he got interested in brewing in the first place.

He's happy to be in Akron. "Akron has had a little resurgence, a little renaissance in brewing lately and we're happy to be part of it," he said, referring to other local breweries Thirsty Dog and Hoppin' Frog.

When it comes to the actual beer, Chris said everyone should enjoy at least one of the Ohio beers. He's proud that several of his beers have won "people's choice" awards at various events. Chris said he's not afraid to make high-alcohol or highly hopped beers, but his regular lineup focuses more on drinkable beers, including the Verich Gold, a kolsch.

"What is wrong with a kolsch?" he asked. "It's a light, drinkable ale. It's a great style. It's a very tough beer to make, because it's unforgiving. Because it doesn't have a lot of hops, relatively speaking, and a lot of malt, you better make it clean, otherwise you can taste the imperfections. I'm very proud that's one of our staples, our Verich Gold."

In addition to the Verich Gold, the regular Ohio Brewing lineup features Cardinal Ale, O'Hoppy Ale, Alt-ernative Amber, and Steel Valley Stout. The brewery also makes many seasonal beers, including Ohio Fest and Jingle Bell Ale.

"I want people to have choices," Chris said. "I usually liken it to you go to an Italian restaurant and they don't have just one pasta. Just ravioli. There's linguini or cavatelli or spaghetti or mostaccioli."

Ohio Brewing beer also can be found downtown at Canal Park, the home of the Akron Aeros baseball team. The Aeroes are the AA affiliate of the Cleveland Indians.

Ohio Brewing Company

Opened: 1997.

Owner: Chris Verich.

Brewer: Chris Verich serves as brewing operations manager.

System: 15-barrel Bohemian Breweries system.

Production: 1,000 barrels.

Distribution: Northeast Ohio.

Hours: The brewery is not open to the public.

Take-out beer: Growlers and kegs.

Tours: Upon request.

Parking: On-street parking.

Other area beer sites: See page 54.

Rust Belt Brewing Company

530 Mahoning Ave., Suite A, Youngstown, OH 44502
330-318-9563 • www.rustybrew.com

Ken Blair wanted a name for his brewery that reflected toughness and a strong work ethic. It can't get much tougher than Rust Belt Brewing Company. The term "Rust Belt" describes the waning manufacturing section of the country that includes Youngstown and Ohio. It's the steel mills and the auto industry. But it's more than that.

Rust Belt depicts hardworking people who have no problem with manual labor, and making beer at a small production brewery—while fun—is hard work, especially for Blair, who has a full-time job as a police officer with the Youngstown Police Department and is one of three owners.

"Partly why we named it Rust Belt is because we put in the same work ethic that these steelworkers do," he said. "There have been some nights when we didn't want to come in here but we do it. We strive to maintain the same type of quality they put into their work."

The Rust Belt theme—the brewery slogan is "Get Rusted"—can be found even in the beer labels, which are dark and moody with images that you'd expect to see in modern comic books. The label for Old Man Hopper's India Pale Ale is the Pittsburgh skyline with a black haze hanging overhead. Then there's the Rusted River Irish Red Ale that features a refinery with hazy orange and red colors.

Rust Belt Brewing is located just outside the heart of downtown Youngstown, a community of about eighty thousand people that has struggled with crime and unemployment since the American steel industry hit hard times. At one point, Youngstown was producing the second-largest amount of steel in the country, behind only Pittsburgh.

The brewery is in the B&O Station Banquet Hall, a gorgeous stone building that sits along the railroad tracks and was once a railroad station. The facility was constructed in 1905 and is listed in the National Register of Historic Places. It also sits along the banks of the Mahoning River in a park-like setting.

Rust Belt is strictly a production brewery. There is no restaurant or food, but people can visit and stop by the Boxcar Lounge next door. The bar serves all the Rust Belt beers.

Up until 2005, the B&O Station served as the community's Amtrak station. Every twenty minutes, a train still rumbles by. The brewery occupies just a small section of the building. The remainder serves as a banquet hall for special events such as weddings and large parties.

Blair had spent time in the U.S. Army and was stationed in Germany and in the Pacific Northwest. That's where he grew to appreciate beer. When he moved to Youngstown, he realized there weren't local breweries making the kind of beer he enjoyed.

"It just tastes better than what you were getting domestically," he said about the beer in Germany and the Pacific Northwest. "It had flavor."

Owning his own brewery had always been in the back of Blair's mind. In 2008, he started homebrewing and approached partners Nick Rosich and Dan McCarthy about starting up their own brewery in Youngstown. The original goal was to make session beers that didn't go crazy with the hops or alcohol content. Instead, they wanted flavorful beers that appealed to the folks drinking national brands. Many breweries have gone over the top with hops and alcohol, and session beers seem to be a lost art today.

Beers brewed: Year-round: Rusted River Irish Red Ale, Blast Furnace Blond, Coke Oven Stout, Old Man Hopper's India Pale Ale, St. Michael's Double Pale Ale, XOXO Doppelsticke Alt Beer, and McPoyle's Milk Stout.

The Pick: The Rusted River Irish Red Ale has a deep copper color. At 5.5 percent alcohol, this is definitely a session beer with a slight initial malt flavor and slight hoppy finish.

"We wanted something that [beer drinkers] can sit there and drink all night," former brewer Lee Gidley said. "We don't want to sell someone one beer, we want to sell them a case."

Blair agreed: "With as many microbreweries out there, you have to find a way to stand out in a market that's getting slightly flooded. There are only so many craft beer drinkers. It's growing rapidly—thank God it's growing rapidly—but we appeal to both the American macro lager drinker and the craft session drinker, too."

Despite that initial goal, Rust Belt, which sells its beer in 22-ounce bottles, has expanded its lineup to include a specialty line with more complex flavors and higher alcohol. That doesn't mean Rust Belt is abandoning its session beer attitude, Blair said, but it had to grow because of the tastes and demands of customers.

The brewery added the John Young Select brand, which includes St. Michael's Double Pale Ale, XOXO Doppelsticke, and McPoyle's Milk Stout.

"It's almost like having two breweries," Blair said.

Rust Belt Brewing Company

Opened: 2008.

Owners: Ken Blair, Nick Rosich, and Dan McCarthy.

Brewers: Nick Rosich and Ken Blair.

System: 10-barrel Criveller system.

Production: 1,000 barrels.

Distribution: Ohio, Pennsylvania, Indiana, Michigan, North Carolina, and South Carolina.

Hours: Thursday and Friday, noon to 8 P.M.; Saturday, noon to 5 P.M.

Tours: Saturday, noon to 5 P.M.

Take-out beer: Bottles and growlers.

Parking: There is plenty of parking outside the building.

Other area beer sites: See page 54.

Thirsty Dog Brewing Company

529 Grant Street, Akron, OH 44311
(330) 252-2739 • www.thirstydog.com

Brewery co-owner John Najeway is proud of plenty of things when it comes to Thirsty Dog. There's the sterling reputation that the brewery has earned for the quality of its beer. There's the day the first bottle rolled off the line after years of operating as a brewpub. And then there's the brewery itself.

Thirsty Dog is located in a redbrick complex that once housed the Burkhart Brewing Company, a family operation and Akron giant that closed in the late 1960s. The brewery, located within walking distance of the University of Akron and about a mile from the heart of downtown Akron, had sat empty for decades when Thirsty Dog opened up shop in 2007.

Najeway and his partners retrofitted the basement for their operation and have their administrative offices in a portion of the first floor. They also opened a small tasting room where people can come in and sample everything they brew. The tasting room also offers select area products, including cheeses made with the brewery's Siberian Night beer.

Thirsty Dog is a production brewery with a massive kettle, giant fermenters, and a bottling line. The operation takes up only a small sliver of the former brewery, which was spread over a couple of brick buildings.

"To actually be in one of the old brewery buildings as an adaptive reuse has been great," said Najeway, whose office is filled with breweriana ranging from beer signs to tap handles. "It makes the story all that much better for the beer lovers . . . and it's really a good marketing tool for us."

People can walk into the brewery anytime during regular hours and pick up a growler, six-pack, or keg. And that happens. Some old-timers have

Beers brewed: Year-round: Orthus Belgian Dubbel, Hoppus Maximus, Cerberus Belgian Tripel, Labrador Lager, Old Leghumper, Raspberry Ale, Siberian Night, Stud Service Stout, Mug Ale, Twisted Kilt, IIPPAA, Lock 3 Lager, and Bourbon Barrel Aged Siberian Night. The brewery also makes seasonal beers.

The Pick: A real tough choice, because of the variety and quality. But how could it not be Siberian Night, a thick Russian imperial stout that has won a gold and two bronze medals at the Great American Beer Festival. At 9 percent alcohol, it's not for the weak.

stopped by and regaled Najeway with stories of how they used to come to Burkhardt Brewing with their fathers and they found it special to revisit the place.

Thirsty Dog ended up in Akron after years of being brewed elsewhere. The brewery started out in 1997 as a brewpub in Canton and then expanded into Centerville and Akron. It quickly earned a solid reputation for its beer thanks to brewer Fred Karm, who won numerous national medals for his recipes. He now runs his own well-respected brewery in Akron: Hoppin' Frog Brewery.

By May 2005, the brewpubs had closed. Najeway, a former homebrewer whose background was in accounting and engineering, had always focused on the beer side of the business. So when the brewpubs shut down, Thirsty Dog already was being made on contract by Frederick Brewing Company in Maryland.

As an Akron native, Najeway wanted to come back to his hometown and he was thrilled to be able to bring craft beer to the community. Thirsty Dog has thrived in Akron. It's now available in eleven states along the East Coast and Midwest. Najeway would like to expand more, but stay just east of the Mississippi River. He has no plans to go national.

"That's one of the reasons we've survived through it all," he said, referring to the demise of other microbreweries. "We've kept a regional footprint."

The brewery produces sixteen different beers, most of them available in both draft and bottle. Most have a dog in the name or on the packaging. For example, there's 12 Dogs of Christmas, Whippet Wheat, and Stud Service Stout.

The flagship beer, which has been around since the beginning, is Old Leghumper, a robust porter and winner of a gold and bronze medal at the World Beer Cup. A close second in sales is Labrador Lager, a traditional German lager.

During my visit, the brewery had just started to devote an entire room to barrel aging in both bourbon barrels and different wine barrels, such as pinot noir for sour beers. The barrels will give Thirsty Dog a new line of beers that are made in small batches and hand-bottled in 750-milliliter bottles, Najeway said.

Thirsty Dog also makes Roobrew beer on contract. Roobrew LLC was the brainchild of Barry Rosenbaum, Gordon Schorr, and John Myers, who provide economic development assistance to the University of Akron. They wanted to start a brewery and decided to go the contract route. The university's mascot is a kangaroo named Zippy, and they decided to name their new operation Roobrew because the community was going bananas over Zippy at the time.

Najeway is passionate about his product and the industry. He's out every week at beer events meeting drinkers face-to-face and pushing the Thirsty Dog brand.

He even started an annual craft beer festival, Blues & Brews, at Akron's Stan Hywet Hall and Gardens, a country estate built by F. A. Seiberling, the founder of the Goodyear Tire & Rubber Company. About three thousand people have attended each year and sipped beer in the shadow of the Manor House, described as "one of the most important historic estates" remaining from the American Country Estate boom in the 1920s. But as of this writing, the festival was moving from Stan Hywet to a new location that hadn't been picked yet.

And as if that weren't enough, Najeway also is the co-founder and head of the Ohio Craft Brewers Association, a group of brewers who organized to bring more attention to locally produced beer. The Blues & Brews festival, traditionally held at the beginning of August, has become a showcase for Ohio beer.

"That is our business," Najeway said. "That's why we're here—to meet people and share what we make. When you lose that passion, you're just another brewer."

Thirsty Dog Brewing Company

Opened: February 1997 as a brewpub. Began contract brewing in 2003 and opened the brewery in 2007.

Owners: John Najeway, Ulo Konsen, and V. Erik Konsen.

Brewer: Tim Rastetter.

System: Century 15-barrel system.

Production: 15,000 barrels a year.

Distribution: Ohio, Maine, Rhode Island, New York, Maryland, Pennsylvania, Kentucky, Michigan, Indiana, Illinois, and North Carolina.

Hours: Monday through Friday, 8 A.M. to 6 P.M. The tasting room is open Wednesday, Thursday, and Friday from 4 P.M. to 8 P.M. and Saturday from 2 P.M. to 6 P.M.

Tours: Saturday at 3 P.M.

Take-out beer: Six-packs, growlers, and kegs.

Food: Thirsty Dog is a production brewery and there's no food service, although the facility can be rented out for parties with catered food.

Parking: A small lot is located next to the brewery.

Other area beer sites: See page 54.

Willoughby Brewing Company

4057 Erie Street, Willoughby, OH 44094
440-975-0202 • www.willoughbybrewing.com

Peanut butter and jelly go together. Peanut butter and beer? The answer, thanks to Willoughby Brewing Company, is an emphatic yes. The brewpub in downtown Willoughby makes one of the most unusual beers in Ohio: Peanut Butter Coffee Porter.

Former brewer Jason Sims loved to experiment with different kinds of beans—coffee beans and vanilla beans, among them. Then he stumbled upon a bean that helped create the signature beer—a peanut butter-flavored coffee bean from Caruso's Coffee in Cleveland. The beer has a remarkable coffee aroma and flavor followed by just a hint of peanut butter.

A new ownership group took over the brewpub in early 2011 and opted—fortunately for beer lovers—to keep making the peanut butter beer. On top of that, the new owners recognized how popular the beer is and decided to start brewing it year-round. Before, it was just available every so often.

One of the goals, co-owner Jeremy Van Horn said, is to put an emphasis back on the beer. Owners Van Horn, Bobby George, and Nika McNulty (whose brother Sam McNulty co-owns the Bier Markt in Cleveland and is co-owner of the Market Garden Brewery) were always big craft beer fans.

"When I was seventeen years old, there were two things I wanted to do: own a bunch of horses and brew beer," McNulty said. She and her husband bought a small horse farm just before buying the brewpub.

"She's living the dream now," Van Horn said, laughing.

For many travelers, just finding Willoughby Brewing might be a challenge. The one-story, red-brick building sits off the main street behind a set of shops in downtown Willoughby, an eastern suburb of Cleveland with about twenty-three thousand people.

Beers brewed: Year-round: Lost Nation Pale Ale, Hop Jam IPA, ToeHead Blond Ale, Railway Razz, and Peanut Butter Coffee Porter. The brewery also has several rotating and seasonal beers on at any given time.

The Pick: The Peanut Butter Coffee Porter is so unusual that you have to get this one. It's a porter made with a peanut butter-flavored coffee bean. The beer has both a strong aroma and flavor of coffee with just a hint of peanut butter.

If you're not looking closely enough or don't know where you're headed, it's easy to miss the place.

The downtown area is the classic American downtown, with storefronts and restaurants lining both sides of the street. It's also become a mini beer mecca, with the 1899 Pub and Nickleby's Roundbar & Kitchen, which both feature substantial beer menus.

The Willoughby Brewing building is a former passenger railroad car repair shop along a Cleveland-to-Ashtabula rail line. It's long and narrow, but still covers 10,000 square feet. If you look closely enough, you can see red steel girders and yellow cranes near the ceiling that were once used in the repair operation.

Willoughby takes the historical aspect of the building seriously. There are plenty of old black-and-white photographs of the structure, which is more than one hundred years old. Beer labels from long-ago Cleveland-area breweries are painted on the walls, and there's also a hobby-size train that runs along a circular track suspended from the ceiling. The train chugs slowly around the track whenever the brewpub is open, carrying cars that contain advertisements for area businesses. There also are plenty of flat-screen televisions around the brewpub.

Most of the space is devoted to dining, with both booths and tables. The bar and area where bands perform are off to one side away from the main dining. The brewhouse, as with most brewpubs, is behind glass just beyond the bar.

Willoughby is supported well by the local community, especially for the live entertainment on the weekends. The brewpub also hosts beer pairing dinners and special tasting events.

During my visit, brewers Rick Seibt and Thomas Gaboury were still refining and tweaking recipes and trying to determine which beers would become regulars. They want to make the styles most popular among craft beer drinkers. So that means, Seibt said, that there will be India pale ales and double IPAs available.

"We want to embrace more of the West Coast styles, more of the styles that are right now popular. But we also want to make sure that we make some good entry-level beers like every brewpub has to," Seibt said.

The brewpub has ten taps, so there's plenty of opportunity. Willoughby Brewing also was interested in starting to distribute its beer—something it hadn't done much of in the past.

A beer that is obviously staying—in addition to the peanut butter one—is Railway Razz. That beer helped put Willoughby Brewing on the map. Railway Razz won three medals at the Great American Beer Festival in the late 1990s and early 2000s.

There also will be cask-conditioned beers available, Seibt said.

Willoughby Brewing Company

Opened:1998.

Owners: Nika McNulty, Jeremy Van Horn, and Bobby George.

Brewer: Rick Seibt and Thomas Gaboury.

System: 15-barrel JV Northwest system.

Production: 900 to 1,200 barrels.

Distribution: At the brewpub and at Eastlake Stadium, where the Lake County Captains professional baseball team plays.

Hours: Sunday through Wednesday, 11 A.M. to midnight; Thursday through Saturday, 11 A.M. to 2 A.M.

Tours: Upon request.

Take-out beer: Growlers.

Food: The menu ranges from regular appetizers to pizzas and burgers.

Extras: The brewpub offers live entertainment on Friday and Saturday nights.

Parking: There is a large lot outside the restaurant.

Other area beer sites: See page 54.

Ohio Craft Brewers Association

Many states have big, strong brewers guilds. What's a brewers guild? It's just a fancy term for a statewide, nonprofit association made up of breweries. The group not only promotes the industry, but also keeps an eye on state legislation to make sure that brewers get represented at the state capital.

For example, Michigan has the Michigan Brewers Guild, Pennsylvania has the Pennsylvania Brewers Guild, Indiana has the Brewers of Indiana Guild, Colorado has the Colorado Brewers Guild . . . you get the picture. Each even operates a website dedicated to the craft industry.

For years, Ohio had two guilds. One focused on the northern part of the state; the other kept an eye on the southern portion. But they both fizzled out, because there was a shake-up in the late 1990s and early 2000s when many Ohio breweries went out of business. The new Ohio Craft Brewers Association was formed in 2008.

John Najeway, association president and one of the owners of Thirsty Dog Brewing in Akron, said, "States around us like Michigan and Pennsylvania that are great craft brewing states, they have strong guilds or associations that give a collaborative voice to the breweries." He continued, "both in talking with the state about legislative issues, and promoting in the retail market the 'Buy local, think local, drink local' theme." One of the big reasons for forming the group involved a state proposal in 2007 that would have ended growler sales. Brewers across the state realized they needed to band together and protect their interests in Columbus. Fortunately, the growler proposal died.

"We don't seem to really get a fair shake from the state of Ohio compared to the wine industry," said Chris Alltmont, brewer at the Gordon Biersch restaurant in Columbus. The brewers realized "unless we organize, we're never going to be able to address these inequities."

So what are these so-called inequities? If you talk to enough Ohio brewers, you'll hear them. The Ohio Division of Liquor Control sells annual permits to make beer and wine. The "A1" permit to manufacture beer costs $3,906 a year. Meanwhile, the "A2" permit to make wine costs $76.

The Ohio Craft Brewers Association has created its own website, www.ohiocraftbrewers.org, highlighting all the breweries in the state. The goals, Najeway said, are to serve as a lobbying group for state legislation and to market craft brewing in the state. The association also sponsors beer festivals and was working to develop a beer trail similar to wine trails for the state.

"I would love to see Ohio, between the wine industry and the beer industry, start getting more credit," said Tony Debevc Jr., the brewer at Cellar Rats Brewery and vice president of operations at Debonne Vineyards, an estate winery in Madison. "You always hear Denver and California. That's with the beer. And then with wine you hear New York, California."

Chris Verich, owner of Ohio Brewing in Akron, agreed, saying: "We want to grow Ohio craft breweries. We want to popularize Ohio craft brewers and be like Oregon and become part of the tourism industry."

Central Ohio

Columbus—well, all of central Ohio—bows down to Ohio State University football. Want to go to a grocery store and have the place all to yourself? Just do it during an Ohio State football game. No, seriously. The entire community, except for bars and restaurants, seems to shut down at game time.

It should come as no surprise considering the university has more than twenty-six thousand workers and is one the top five largest employers in Ohio. Add in more than sixty-four thousand students—not counting graduates—and that's a lot of loyal Ohio State fans.

For years, Ohio State football was the only game in town. Despite being one of the largest cities in the United States, with a population of more than 730,000 people, Columbus had no professional sports. If you grew up here and were interested in the NFL or Major League Baseball, you looked to Cleveland or Cincinnati.

Columbus finally got its first major professional sports franchise in 2000 when the Columbus Blue Jackets hockey team arrived. Others would argue that the Blue Jackets, who stunk for years, didn't actually arrive until 2009 when they first qualified for the playoffs. The Blue Jackets play at Nationwide Arena, which holds 18,500 people for hockey and up to 20,000 for concerts. The Gordon Biersch brewpub is located in the arena district.

For soccer fans, the city also has been home to Major League Soccer since the mid-1990s. The Columbus Crew even have their own soccer-specific stadium that seats more than twenty thousand.

But no matter how many professional sports teams are brought in, Columbus will always be known for Ohio State football. Because the university is based in the city and Columbus serves as the state capital, the community has fared better than other Ohio cities when it comes to the local economy.

Government jobs, including those at the university, always seem to be more stable than those in the private sector. There are more than government employees living and working in Columbus, though. Fortune 500 companies Nationwide Mutual Insurance, American Electric Power, Limited Brands, and Big Lots are all headquartered here.

Other mid-sized communities that ring the city—Mansfield, Newark, Springfield, and Zanesville—all are overshadowed by the state capital, which as I mentioned before is overshadowed by Ohio State football.

Columbus is flush with highways. There are Interstates 71, 70, 270, and 670. Conceivably, you'd think it'd be easy to travel around with so many routes available. Alas, it is not. The metro region is also flush with people—more than 1 million of them. And for some reason, they always seem to be on the highway. (They also seem to be getting into accidents all the time!)

Never, never, never . . . and I repeat never . . . try to drive around Columbus during rush hour. Many of my trips to Columbus or farther south included me stopped in highway traffic, alternating between resting my head on the steering wheel while I sobbed and swearing up a storm at the idiot drivers around me.

Central Ohio has a rich beer heritage, but really is still finding its place in the craft beer movement. Anheuser-Busch has been making beer in Columbus since 1968. Columbus Brewing Company, which opened in 1988, is one of the oldest microbreweries in the state but has never really garnered the accolades of Cleveland's Great Lakes Brewing Company, which opened just a few months before it. Many craft breweries are just starting to spring up in the community, and those brewers admit that the area has a long way to go in terms of promoting craft beer.

Here's a look at some beer-related sites to visit while traveling through Central Ohio.

- **BJ's Restaurant & Brewhouse** (1414 Polaris Parkway, Columbus, 614-885-1800, www.bjsbrewhouse.com) is part of a corporate chain based in Huntington Beach, California. BJ's offers plenty of house beers, including several that have won medals at the Great American Beer Festival. The Columbus location doesn't actually brew beer on the premises and instead gets its BJ's beers delivered. (See the "A Word About . . . Other Breweries" on page 141 for more about BJ's, which also has a location in Cincinnati.)

- **The Winking Lizard restaurants** (www.winkinglizard.com) have been recommended previously in this book as great places to get a beer. Well, there are two located in Columbus at 1380 Bethel Road and 100 Hutchinson Avenue.

- **The Surly Girl Saloon** (1126 N. High Street, Columbus, 614-294-4900, www.surlygirlsaloon.com) is a little hole in the wall near Ohio State. Any bar that carries Piraat and Abbaye des Rocs Grand Cru alongside Pabst Blue Ribbon and Miller High Life is a place worth checking out.

- **Bodega** (1044 N. High Street, Columbus, 614-299-9399, www.columbusbodega.com) offers more than fifty beers on draft and more than one hundred in bottles, including an impressive list of seasonals. The menu includes appetizers, paninis, and pizzas.

- **Mellow Mushroom** (2170 Polaris Parkway, Columbus, 614-885-6355, www.mellowmushroom.com) offers more than one hundred beers in bottles and on draft. Red Brick Brewing Company in Atlanta makes a special Mellow Mushroom Bogart Pale Ale for the chain restaurant, which specializes in pizzas.

- **The German Village** downtown (www.germanvillage.com) always pops up as a must-visit for beer fans. At one time, the area, which is listed in the National Register of Historic Places, was home to the community's German population and multiple breweries. Today, it's a redeveloped neighborhood filled with redbrick buildings, brick-paved streets, restaurants, bars, and homes. Columbus Brewing Company is located in this neighborhood.

  Those wanting a taste of Germany while visiting the German Village should make a stop at **Schmidt's Restaurant und Sausage Haus** (240 E. Kossuth Street, Columbus, 614-444-6808, www.schmidthaus.com), which serves up traditional German dishes, such as wiener schnitzel, chicken spaetzle, and sauerbraten and gravy. Other adventurous eaters will want to visit the **The Thurman Café** (183 Thurman Avenue, Columbus, 614-443-1570, www.thethurmancafe.com) for a famous 3/4-pound Thurman Burger.

Here are some other recommended attractions in the area.

- **The Columbus Zoo and Aquarium** (4850 W. Powell Road, Powell, 614-645-3550, www.colszoo.org) is visited by more than two million people each year and has been rated the top zoo in the country by the online site *USA Travel Guide*. There are more than seven thousand animals here, but the zoo's longtime director Jack

Hanna is more famous than all of them. He's appeared on countless television entertainment programs, including *The Late Show* with David Letterman, and has hosted his own shows to promote wildlife and conservation efforts. Hanna has become so popular he even has his own website (www.jackhanna.com).

- **The Jack Nicklaus Museum** (2355 Olentangy River Road, Columbus, 614-247-5959, www.nicklausmuseum.org). Many beer drinkers enjoy golf and one of the greatest golfers in history just happens to be from Columbus. This museum is home to all things Nicklaus. Located in The Ohio State University sports complex, it features a collection of golf memorabilia in a 24,000-square-foot building.

- **The Motorcycle Hall of Fame Museum** (13515 Yarmouth Drive, Pickerington, 614-856-2222, www.motorcyclemuseum.org) was founded in 1990 by the American Motorycle Heritage Foundation. The museum pays tribute to motorcycle enthusiasts and offers rotating exhibits.

- **The Short North Arts District** (614-299-8050, www.shortnorth .org) is an area just north of downtown Columbus that's filled with art galleries, specialty shops, bars, and restaurants. The **Greater Columbus Convention Center** is here too. Barley's Brewing Company, Ale House No. 1 also is located in the area and Gordon Biersch is just down the street, so you're bound to end up in this neighborhood at some point if you're visiting Ohio breweries.

- **The Longaberger Company's Home Office** (1500 E. Main Street, Newark). If goofy roadside attractions are your thing, then you have to take a swing through Newark, home to the basketmaker Longaberger. The corporate headquarters is a seven-story building that looks exactly like a giant basket.

- **The Longaberger Homestead** (5563 Raiders Road, Frazeysburg, 740-322-5588, www.longaberger.com) is the place to see the basket making in action.

- **The Y-Bridge**. Speaking of goofy, Zanesville has an unusual y-shaped bridge, first opened in 1814, that spans the confluence of the Muskingum and Licking Rivers. It is a famous landmark, with aviator Amelia Earhart once calling Zanesville the most recognizable city in the country because the span was so visible from the air.

- **The Wilds** (14000 International Road, Cumberland, 740-638-5030, www.thewilds.org) is a nonprofit organization and conservation

area covering nearly 10,000 acres. It's considered one of the largest conservation centers in North America and home to hundreds of species, including rhinos and giraffes. More than seventy-five thousand people take safari tours through the center each year.

Barley's Brewing Company, Ale House No. 1

ALE HOUSE NO. 1

467 N. High Street, Columbus, OH 43215
614-228-2537 • www.barleysbrewing.com

The craft brewing industry can be quite volatile. Small breweries open just as fast as they close, and brewers tend to bounce around quite a bit looking for their perfect fit.

Barley's is unusual. Until 2011, brewmaster Scott Francis and head brewer Angelo Signorino have been with the brewpub since its inception in 1992, and they helped launch a second location a few miles away in 1998. They were the longest-tenured brewers at any single operation in Ohio. Asked in late 2010 how that made him feel, Francis shrugged and responded, "Old."

Francis, who left Barley's in early 2011 and handed over the brewmaster reins to Signorino, is sort of a grandfather in the beer industry. He opened a homebrewing and wine making shop in 1974 in Columbus. He stuck with it until 1988, when he became the original brewer at the Columbus Brewing Company. He left there to join Barley's and has been there ever since, bringing Signorino, a former worker at his homebrew shop, along with him.

Through the years, he also helped set up private breweries at the Atwood Yacht Club, New Albany Country Club, and Hide-a-Way Hills Club and still brews at those locations. After nearly four decades in the field, the talkative Francis has plenty of wisdom, humor, and observations to share.

Beers brewed: Year-round: Barley's Pilsner, MacLenny's Scottish Ale, and Barley's Pale Ale. An India pale ale and stout are always on tap too, but the recipes change. There usually are seven or eight Barley beers on tap. The brewery also makes rotating and seasonal beers.

The Pick: The MacLenny's Scottish Ale is a must for the original Barley's. Francis and Signorino scorch the wort, which provides a nice caramelized color and flavor to the beer.

On making beer: "The hardest beer to make is the first one. Then the second hardest is the hundredth batch."

On what it was like starting out in 1988: "I didn't know what I was doing. But I knew that. That's where a lot of brewers get into trouble in that they don't know what they're doing and they don't know that. They think they know what they are doing. You can tell by the beer. You can tell by their business decisions."

On being a brewmaster: "When you're the brewmaster, it just means you get yelled at more by the owner."

The two Barley's are different in terms of atmosphere and food. They also have different brewhouses, although the same beers—except for one or two—are made at both locations. It's rare for a beer to be shipped from one restaurant to the other. The beer tastes slightly different thanks to the separate systems, even though the same recipes and yeasts are used.

"As far as the beers go, we really try to be authentically British with our ales," Francis said. "I call them very soft. They have a lot of middle to them. We undertone everything. I like stuff to be very understated and very balanced."

Michael Jackson, the late beer writer and traveler, even praised Barley's in one of his early books for making authentic British ales. "In my little world that was awesome to say that I did one of the best in the United States," Francis said.

Barley's uses English malts to obtain that flavor profile, and the yeast originally came from Fuller's in London. Francis and Signorino also enjoy doing cask-conditioned beers and place the firkin right on the bar to be tapped. But that's not to say they don't have fun with some out-of-the-ordinary beers. There's always an American-style India pale ale on tap and they have made a raspberry wheat barleywine, organic mild ale, and Belgian strong ale.

"We do all over the map from session beers to super strong, as strong as Ohio allows," Signorino said.

The original High Street location has more of a pub feel, with a menu focused on high-end bar food. The Ale House No. 1, as it's called, is in the Short North, an arts and cultural neighborhood filled with bars, restaurants, and art galleries, just north of downtown. It sits in a skinny row building across the street from the Greater Columbus Convention Center and benefits from the events there. The interior has a well-worn wooden floor and giant mirror behind the bar, and it is dominated by wooden booths along one of the walls.

First-time visitors also may find something amiss, especially for a brewpub. The brewhouse isn't visible. That's because it's in the basement. Just to the left of the bar is a row of windows where people can peer down to see the brewers at work.

The best-selling beer is the MacLenny's Scottish Ale, which really should be consumed at the original location. Why? Because there's something special about the way it's made there. The kettle has a flat bottom and is heated with direct flame. Signorino fires up the heater and directs 400,000 BTUs at the kettle floor before any wort is even added. After the kettle is hot, he adds about half a barrel of wort. Imagine the sound of an egg dropping onto a blistering hot frying pan.

"It scorches and caramelizes and leaves a nice skid mark that we scrub out at the end of the day," Signorino said. "It gives the beer all its color and caramelly flavor. The character comes from that scorching process. It's a nice beer for people who really like beer but don't want to get anything too extreme. But I wouldn't call it a beer with training wheels at all. It's a sturdy beer."

He called it "beer brûlée," in reference to the popular dessert. It's not a brewing process Signorino and Francis recommend for others. And they can't duplicate it at the Ale House No. 2 because the kettle bottom is slanted there.

"It's not something you tell another brewer that's not familiar with this," Francis said. "You tell them that we turn on our hot kettle empty, they're going to say we're nuts. Which we are."

Barley's does something else different for a brewpub, too. Each year, Francis and Signorino hold a homebrewing competition. The winner gets to come into the brewpub and make their beer on Barley's professional system. The homebrewer also gets to name their beer and design a special tap handle. One year, a blood orange wheat won. The winners also have included Jay Wince, who now owns and brews at Weasel Boy Brewing Company in Zanesville (see page 107).

Barley's Brewing Company, Ale House No. 1

Opened: 1992.

Owner: Lenny Kolada.

Brewer: Angelo Signorino.

System: 10-barrel Century Manufacturing system.

Production: 800 barrels.

Distribution: At the brewpubs and a couple of other select bars in the Columbus area.

Hours: Monday through Thursday, 11 A.M. to midnight; Friday and Saturday, 11 A.M. to 2 A.M.; Sunday, noon to 11 P.M.

Tours: Upon request.

Take-out beer: Growlers.

Food: Higher-end pub food, such as sirloin, pasta, pot roast, burgers, and other sandwiches.

Parking: On-street parking.

Other area beer sites: See page 84.

Barley's Smokehouse & Brewpub, Ale House No. 2

1130 Dublin Road, Columbus, OH 43215
614-485-0227 • www.barleysbrewing.com

The Barley's Dublin Road site, or Ale House No. 2, as it's called, is in a stand-alone building along a busy road. It has a restaurant feel with a menu focused on barbecue. A powerful smoky aroma hits customers when they first walk in. The brewhouse is behind glass and is on the same floor as the bar, so it can be easily seen by customers as they drink their beer.

The bar also features something different. Just above the customers' heads are hundreds of tickets to sporting events and concerts stapled to an overhang. It's fun to look at the tickets to everything from a Columbus Blue Jackets game to the Indianapolis 500.

Scott Francis enjoys brewing at the Ale House No. 2 site a little more. For starters, he doesn't have to lug ingredients up and down stairs. The brewhouse sits at the front of the restaurant and there are large windows allowing in sunlight, as opposed to being in the dungeon-like basement at the original location.

Beers brewed: Year-round: Barley's Pilsner, MacLenny's Scottish Ale, and Barley's Pale Ale. An India pale ale and stout are always on tap too, but the recipes change. There usually are seven or eight Barley beers on tap. The brewery also makes rotating and seasonal beers.

The Pick: The Barley's Pale Ale is a British pale ale made with two-row English barley malt. It has a great balance of malt and hops and is a terrific alternative to the hoppier American pale ales.

Barley's Smokehouse & Brewpub, Ale House No. 2

Opened: 1998.

Owners: Lenny Kolada and Scott Francis.

Brewer: Angelo Signorino.

System: 10-barrel Century Manufacturing system.

Production: 500 barrels.

Distribution: At the brewpubs and a couple of other select bars in the Columbus area.

Hours: Monday through Thursday, 11 A.M. to close; Friday, 11 A.M. to close; Saturday and Sunday, noon to close. The kitchen closes at 11 P.M. Saturday and 8:30 P.M. Sunday.

Tours: Upon request.

Take-out beer: Growlers.

Food: Hickory-smoked meats, such as St. Louis–style ribs and pulled pork. The menu also features burgers and sandwiches.

Parking: Free parking lot.

Other area beer sites: See page 84.

Columbus Brewing Company

535 Short Street, Columbus, OH 43215
614-224-3626 • www.columbusbrewing.com

Baseball player Jackie Robinson gets all the credit for breaking Major League Baseball's color barrier in 1947 with the Brooklyn Dodgers. Few remember the second black player in the big leagues: Larry Doby, who joined the Cleveland Indians less than three months later.

So seems to be the fate of Columbus Brewing Company in Columbus. Great Lakes Brewing Company in Cleveland is recognized and spoken of with reverence for being the first craft brewer to open in Ohio in 1988. That same year, though, Columbus Brewing also opened its doors.

"It was neck and neck," brewmaster and owner Eric Bean said.

While Great Lakes has grown and earned national acclaim, the road was a bumpy one for Columbus Brewing. But Bean said the brewery is now focused on growing and cementing its own stellar reputation in the beer industry.

In 2010, Columbus Brewing picked up its first Great American Beer Festival medal—a bronze for its Summer Teeth in the kellerbier/zwickelbier category. The brewery also branched out that year by developing the "Hop Odyssey" program, which involved a line of limited-edition hoppy beers. A new one was released each month. It was such a success that Bean said he planned to do similar monthly releases each year.

"We're trying to grow into a statewide brand and that's our focus," Bean said. "As we learn, we know we have to have the pale ale and IPA—those beers that you can sit down and drink a six-pack in a night. That's what's going to pay the bills. But we also are trying to put out some of those beers that garnish attention but are still really drinkable."

Columbus Brewing is located in the city's Brewery District, an area just off Interstate 70 filled with redbrick warehouses that have been converted into condos, restaurants, bars, and businesses. With a name like the Brewery District, it should come as no surprise that the area has a rich history of brewing. The district was home to five breweries over the years, including City Brewery and Capitol Breweries.

Columbus Brewing is an odd duck in the industry. There is a Columbus Brewing restaurant and a Columbus Brewing brewery. The two are separate businesses but share the same modern, Art Deco building, which really stands out from the brick former warehouses. The beer also is available at the restaurant, which serves American fare ranging from pizza to meatloaf to orange-glazed salmon.

While many people might think Columbus Brewing is a brewpub, it's really a production brewery—and a large one at that, with a 30-barrel system. The brewery both bottles its beer and has it available on draft in locations throughout the Columbus market.

Bean arrived in 2005 after stints with breweries in Cleveland, San Francisco, and Seattle. He has an interesting background for a brewer. He graduated from Kent State University with a degree in biological anthropology, which involves the study of human evolution.

"I really thought brewing was going to be something between undergraduate and graduate school," Bean said.

But he ended up enjoying the beer industry so much—and not enjoying the politics of academics—that he stuck with brewing. A graduate of the University of California at Davis brewing program,

Beers brewed: Year-round: Pale Ale, IPA, Scottish Ale, and 1859 Porter. The brewery also makes seasonal and rotating beers, including Summer Teeth, which won a bronze medal at the Great American Beer Festival.

The Pick: The Summer Teeth, an unfiltered kellerbier, won a bronze medal at the 2010 Great American Beer Festival. It's crisp and light. It's a seasonal offering, so if it's not available, check out the Scottish Ale, which is heavy on the malt flavor.

Bean said his approach to creating beer is to make sure each beer is well-balanced.

"They are dry. They're very approachable beers," he said. "Even our bigger beers—I focus on the fact that you can drink several of them. I think it comes from studying with a German brewmaster, and the idea is that you should be able to drink them and it's not about some profound flavor. It's about enjoying an entire pint."

Columbus Brewing Company

Opened: 1988.

Owner: Eric Bean.

Brewer: Eric Bean.

System: 30-barrel Creveller system.

Production: 3,200 barrels.

Distribution: At the Columbus Brewing restaurant and throughout the Columbus market in grocery stores, bars, and restaurants. The brewery also is expanding distribution statewide.

Hours: The brewery is not open to the public. The restaurant is open Monday through Thursday, 11 A.M. to 10 P.M.; Friday, 11 A.M. to 11 P.M.; and Saturday, 5 P.M. to 11 P.M.

Tours: None.

Take-out beer: Growlers.

Extras: Bean created A Hop Odyssey in 2010. It involves releasing a new hoppy beer on draft each month. He plans to do similar limited, monthly programs in future years.

Food: The restaurant has an extensive menu that includes appetizers, sandwiches, salads, and main dishes, such as meatloaf, pecan-crusted chicken, and Cajun jambalaya.

Parking: There is plenty of parking in the restaurant lot.

Other area beer sites: See page 84.

Elevator Brewery & Draught Haus

161 N. High Street, Columbus, OH 43215
614-228-0500 • www.elevatorbrewing.com

Dick Stevens can sure tell an entertaining story. Make that stories. There's the one about how he and his son Ryan got into the brewery and restaurant business with absolutely no brewing or restaurant experience, other than being big drinkers, of course.

Or how his son cracked the Columbus market. Ryan would go into bars and sell a keg with the understanding that if it wasn't kicked by a certain time of the night, it'd be free. Then, he and his buddies would descend upon the joint and drink it dry.

And, of course, there's the time Dick Stevens came up with an idea for a beer—a mocha plum stout—and decided that he should help brew it. He did. That was the first and last time he's ever brewed.

"I've already retired, because I figure I can't do any better," laughed Dick, who carried on the Elevator operation after his son died suddenly in 2003. "I hit a winner. The downside is I could brew again and it would be horrible. So I quit on top. A one-brew wonder."

Stevens, whose business card lists him as "elevator operator" and "dictator," is having fun. He is one of the most entertaining personalities in the Ohio brewing industry. You can even see it in Elevator's cartoon beer labels. The hefeweizen is called Heiferweizen and the label is a big fat cow in lederhosen hoisting a beer mug. And the barrel-aged porter, called Horny Goat, has a goat ready to mount a beer bottle.

"Our mission statement—well it's not really an official mission statement—is to elevate people's taste with big, bold beers without taking ourselves too seriously," he said. "This is a fun business and we have fun. I think the most rewarding thing is to see people drinking good beer."

Elevator Brewing was born in 1999 in Marysville, about a half hour northwest of Columbus.

Beers brewed: Year-round: Dark Horse Lager, Bleeding Buckeye Red Ale, Three Frogs IPA, Bear Ass Pale Ale, Dirty Dick's Nut Brown Ale, Procrastinator Doppelbock, Xtra Lager, Fly'n Hydrant Light, and Mogabi American Wheat. The brewery also offers rotating and seasonal beers.

The Pick: Dark Horse Lager won a bronze medal at the 2007 Great American Beer Festival. It's a tasty, lightly hopped brown lager that's easy drinking at 5.3 percent alcohol.

The brewery, along with a restaurant, was built inside a grain elevator. Thus the name Elevator Brewing.

Dick and Ryan Stevens controlled the brewery and the restaurant was operated separately. They thought they were onto something in Marysville because of the industry located there, including Honda of America, and a lack of nice restaurants. But the restaurant side of the business never worked out.

They decided to open their own restaurant in 2000 in downtown Columbus in a former pool hall and gentlemen's saloon. The building, listed in the National Register of Historic Places, dates back to 1897 when the Bott Bros. Manufacturing Company made bar-backs and pool tables there. Later, the location became a famous pool hall where greats like Minnesota Fats would stop in. The brewpub still has some antique billiard tables, including an eight-foot table from 1891 and a seven-foot table from 1884.

It is the most gorgeous brewpub in Ohio, with its mosaic tile floor, stained glass windows, onyx columns behind the bar, inlaid mother of pearl, carved mahogany wood, and giant artwork hanging on the walls in the dining area. The mahogany bar-back won a blue ribbon for craftsmanship at the 1893 World Columbian Exposition in Chicago. When it was built, there were no bar stools and people literally had to belly up to the bar.

"A lot of people walk into our restaurant and they don't even know we're a brewpub," Stevens said.

When the restaurant opened, the brewery stayed behind in Marysville. It didn't move to Columbus until 2009, when Stevens bought a brick manufacturing building two blocks away from the brewpub. That brewery, operated as a separate business, supplies the restaurant and other draft accounts and also bottles beer. Elevator also brews on contract for Wooden Shoe Brewing in Minster.

Stevens is particularly proud of his "Masters of Beer Appreciation" program. He readily admits he stole the idea, which rewards customers for drinking a special beer brewed each month. Customers get an MBA card and a 25-ounce mug that is filled for life at the 16-ounce price. If they finish all twelve beers in a year, they also receive a diploma for graduating from the program. He estimated that more than one thousand people had gotten diplomas over the first ten years.

As for the beer itself, Elevator makes both big beers and session beers. The brewpub has about twelve house beers on tap at any given time. Asked what his philosophy is when developing beer, Stevens, in his usual humorous way, responded, "I want to sell it because I have to pay the bills."

Elevator Brewery & Draught Haus

Opened: 1999.

Owner: Dick Stevens.

Brewer: Vic Schiltz.

System: 15-barrel North American Brewing system.

Production: 2,000 barrels.

Distribution: On draft and in bottles throughout the Columbus market.

Hours: The restaurant is open Monday through Wednesday, 11 A.M. to midnight; Thursday, 11 A.M. to 1 A.M.; Friday, 11 A.M. to 2 A.M.; and Saturday, 5 P.M. to 2 A.M. The restaurant is closed on Sunday.

Tours: Tours are offered at 4 P.M. the third Saturday of each month at the brewery, 165 N. Fourth Street. The cost is $20 per person and people receive a souvenir pint glass, T-shirt, beer tasting, and free pint at the restaurant.

Take-out beer: Growlers and six-packs.

Food: American fare with a full line of appetizers, salads, and entrees, but it's much more upscale than a regular brewpub menu. Dinners range from filet or tuna served on a Finnish Tulikivi firestone to New York strip to pork tenderloin.

Extras: Elevator offers a "Masters of Beer Appreciation" program. Customers must drink a different, special beer each month for a year to earn their MBA and receive a diploma.

Parking: On-street parking.

Other area beer sites: See page 84.

Gordon Biersch

401 N. Front Street, Columbus, OH 43215
614-24-2901 • www.gordonbiersch.com

Brewer Chris Alltmont takes the Reinheitsgebot, better known as the "German Beer Purity Law," seriously. He has to as a brewer for Gordon Biersch, which focuses on traditional German-style lagers and follows a strict interpretation of the Reinheitsgebot, the law approved in 1516 that required brewers to use only water, barley, and hops in their beer-making. That means the beer is drier and crisper than other breweries that make ales, and you won't find any high-hopped India pale ales or high-alcohol barleywines here.

"A lot of the beers we make . . . are approachable and familiar," Alltmont said. "We are definitely not at the forefront of making extreme beers that push the limits. We are more interested in just trying to make as authentic [German] beers as we can possibly make. The advantage that we have is that we can make them fresher than anything you can bring over from Germany."

Gordon Biersch Brewery Restaurants are part of the CraftWorks Restaurants & Breweries chain, which operates nearly two hundred restaurants under fourteen different names. Those brands include Old Chicago and Rock Bottom. Then there is the Gordon Biersch Brewery in San Jose, California, which makes the same beer available at the brewpubs but bottles it for retail sale. The brewery is operated separately from the restaurant side. But both owe their origins to brewer Dan Gordon and restaurateur Dean Biersch. They opened the first Gordon Biersch restaurant in 1988 in Palo Alto, California.

The Columbus brewpub, opened in 2001, is located downtown in a brick complex filled with restaurants and businesses next to Nationwide Arena, home to the NHL's Columbus Blue Jackets. The arena also hosts events such as the Harlem Globetrotters and Trans-Siberian Orchestra, and can hold up to twenty thousand people for concerts. When there's a hockey game or special event, Gordon Biersch can get quite crowded.

Beers brewed: Year-round: Golden Export, Hefeweizen, Czech Pilsner, Marzen, and Schwarzbier. The brewpub also has a seasonal available at all times.

The Pick: The Czech Pilsner has a nice, spicy hop character thanks to the Saaz hops. It also has a clean, dry finish.

"A lot of our locations you'll find next to sporting venues and then we've got quite a few in large shopping malls and retail areas," Alltmont said.

Despite the brewing equipment being set up at the front of the building and exposed for people to see from the street, plenty of folks still wander in not knowing that Gordon Biersch is a brewery. Perhaps that's because the brewpub is set up more as a traditional chain restaurant. There's a circular bar in one area and the rest of the space is set aside for dining. While the brewery focuses on German beer, there is no German influence when it comes to the menu, which can be described as California cuisine. The restaurant also has an exposed kitchen where people can watch their food be prepared.

As for Gordon Biersch itself, people tend to know two things. The Marzen, a traditional Oktoberfest lager, is the flagship beer and is used in plenty of the restaurant's foods, including the barbecue sauce and vinaigrette. And, of course, the restaurant serves garlic fries, which Dan Gordon created.

"That's really the cornerstone the company is built on," Alltmont said about the garlic fries, laughing.

Because Gordon Biersch is a national chain, the beer offered in Columbus also tends to be the same offered in Chicago or Miami. But brewers at each location also produce special seasonal offerings.

In addition to taking the Reinheitsgebot seriously, Gordon Biersch also is focused on quality. The company is a frequent winner at the Great American Beer Festival and World Beer Cup, with the Schwarzbier, Czech Pilsner, Weizenbock, Eisbock, Dunkel, Golden Export, Altbier, Hefeweizen, Rauchbier, and SommerFest all picking up medals since 2007.

Alltmont, who had worked at several other breweries before coming to Gordon Biersch, said he was surprised about the company's bonus structure for brewers when he first arrived. Instead of basing bonuses on quantity, the company places an emphasis on quality control. Beer from each restaurant is sent off to a lab to be analyzed for quality and bonuses are based on those results.

"We are a big chain that likes to have some consistency and control over things," he said.

Gordon Biersch

Opened: 2001.
Owner: CraftWorks Restaurants & Breweries.
Brewer: Chris Alltmont.

System: 20-barrel Specific Mechanical system.

Production: 1,200 barrels

Hours: Monday through Thursday, 11 A.M. to 11 P.M.; Friday and Saturday, 11 A.M. to 1 A.M.; and Sunday, 11 A.M. to 10 P.M.

Tours: Upon request.

Take-out beer: Growlers and kegs.

Food: The brewpub has a full menu, best described as California cuisine. Items range from appetizers to sandwiches to dinners, including steak and seafood.

Extras: Gordon Biersch offers Passports Reward and Stein Club programs that allow customers to accrue points and then redeem them for merchandise and vacations. The brewpub also offers special beer-pairing dinners. The restaurant also has a location at Cleveland Hopkins International Airport, but there's no brewing done there.

Parking: On-street parking.

Other area beer sites: See page 84.

Hide-A-Way Hills Lodge and Microbrewery

29042 Hide-A-Way Hills Road,
Hide-A-Way Hills, OH 43155
740-569-4195 • www.hide-a-wayhillsclub.com

Hide-A-Way Hills is a sprawling, 1,650-acre private resort in rural southeast Ohio with its own guard shack and gate in front to keep out uninvited visitors. Inside, it's a paradise for members.

It's dotted with about seven hundred homes and cabins, where some people live full time, and filled with five lakes, beaches, horse stables, a nine-hole golf course, shooting range, two post offices, a dirt bike track, and surprisingly, a brewery.

Located about an hour southeast of Columbus and less than a half hour from Lancaster, Hide-A-Way Hills is in a remote wooded area at the end of a winding country road.

Why is a brewery at a private resort in the middle of nowhere? Out of necessity. Hide-A-Way Hills was founded in 1961 as part of a movement across

Beers brewed: Year-round beers: Rushcreek Pale Ale and Rushcreek Lager.

The Pick: The Rushcreek Pale Ale is an English-style pale ale, meaning it has more malt balance than your hoppy American brands. It's quite smooth.

the United States to create beautiful, gated communities. There was one major problem, though, for members who enjoyed drinking alcohol. The club—so large that it spans both Fairfield and Hocking Counties—was in a dry community and alcohol sales weren't permitted.

That posed a significant challenge for the Lodge restaurant, which operated on a thin margin to begin with. Without liquor, it was even tougher to keep the restaurant filled with customers and operating.

Members did their best to try to change that. They even went to voters and placed issues on the ballot to allow alcohol sales. But there was another major problem. Most of the members didn't live at Hide-A-Way Hills full time, so they didn't get to vote, and residents living around there shot the issue down. So the club never could get approval.

"You can't make it without booze. It just can't work," said David Harcum, a retired school superintendent who bought into the resort in 1966 and has lived there full time since 1984.

That doesn't mean members didn't drink alcohol at the Lodge. They drank illegally, as people at many places did back then. One way was bringing your own liquor and keeping it at the restaurant. It was an open secret, Harcum said, as government leaders and even sheriff's officials would visit the restaurant occasionally for an event.

But a disgruntled member called the state Division of Liquor Control in the 1980s and the club was told it needed to operate legally.

Then members heard about a loophole in Ohio law. Business mogul Les Wexner, the founder of such companies as The Limited, Victoria's Secret, and Abercrombie & Fitch, wanted to bring alcohol sales to the New Albany Country Club in suburban Columbus, but the community was dry. He learned that if the club opened a brewery, then it would have a full state liquor permit, Harcum said.

So that's what the country club did. And Hide-A-Way Hills members, led by Harcum, followed suit.

"I got a commitment from a gentleman down here that he would put in X number of dollars and I would put in X number of dollars and we would raise money and start a brewery," Harcum said. "Knowing zero about anything, nothing. But that's never stopped me from doing something just because I didn't know anything."

Harcum, who had raised about $100,000, nosed around to find other breweries and learn what he had to do to turn the idea into reality. He visited Barley's Brewing Company in downtown Columbus and met brewer Scott Francis, who helped them buy a Century Manufacturing system that had been built special for a trade show.

Francis, intrigued by the idea, became the part-time brewer and Hide-A-Way Hills began producing beer in 1993. The Lodge doesn't offer an extensive list of craft beer. It makes only two styles, an English pale ale and a lager. Remember, the brewery is there to serve a purpose of a full liquor license and not there to produce great quantities or experimental styles.

The brewery is attached to the Lodge restaurant. Members donated their time and own money to add the brewhouse onto the building. No club money was used to build the brewhouse—or buy the brewing equipment. The Lodge, as you'd expect in such a rural setting, has a cabin-in-the-woods feel with wooden tables and chairs and a big stone fireplace. Large windows overlook the wooded grounds.

The restaurant, which offers typical American fare, including sandwiches and larger meals, is deep in the resort and it takes a few minutes to drive from the guard shack along winding and hilly roads to reach it. The speed limit is 19 mph. Why? General manager Randy Swetnam said that's just the way it is. That odd speed limit, he added, is designed to catch your attention. Of course, you don't want to drive much faster than that anyway, because of the way the roads twist and turn.

While the club itself is not open to the public, the restaurant is. The club is trying to promote the Lodge more and figures that offering locally made beer can't hurt. The public is welcome to make reservations and visit.

Hide-A-Way Hills Lodge and Microbrewery

Opened: 1993.

Owner: Hide-A-Way Hills Club.

Brewer: Scott Francis.

System: Century Manufacturing.

Distribution: At the restaurant only.

Hours: The restaurant is open Tuesday through Thursday, 5 P.M. to 9 P.M. and Friday and Saturday, 5 P.M. to 10 P.M. The bar is open Tuesday through Thursday, 5 P.M. to 10 P.M. and Friday and Saturday, 5 P.M. to midnight.

Tours: Upon request.

Take-out beer: Growlers.

Food: The restaurant has an extensive menu that includes appetizers, sandwiches, salads, and main dishes, such as prime rib, smoked pork chops, and Maryland crab cakes.

Parking: There is plenty of parking in the restaurant lot across the road.

Other area beer sites: See page 84.

Neil House Brewery

**372 Morrison Road, Suite D,
Columbus, OH 43213
www.neilhousebrewery.com**

Patrick Kelleher had no idea what to call his fledging brewery, so a friend came up with the name. Kelleher, an undergraduate chemistry student at Ohio State University at the time, was homebrewing at his house on Neil Avenue in Columbus, not far from campus. When asked the name of his brewery one day, he stumbled.

Then someone, Kelleher can't remember who, chimed in with "Neil House Brewery." The name stuck and Kelleher couldn't be happier. Columbus has been an important part of his family and the Neil name has been just as important in Columbus history.

In 1870, stagecoach businessman William Neil donated the land that would eventually become home to Ohio State. He constructed a long road, today called Neil Avenue, to get to his farm. Neil also built a tavern called Neil House in 1839 in downtown. It would become the Neil House Hotel, which was torn down in the 1970s.

Kelleher opened the Neil House Brewery & Homebrew Supply in 2010 with the help of friends. The brewery and shop originally was located in a strip mall in Reynoldsburg, but during my visit in late 2010, the operation was moving to an industrial park nearby in Columbus. The brewery was still getting off the ground and the beers weren't yet ready for sampling. The good news is Kelleher planned to have a taproom at the new site so people could taste his beer and get instant feedback.

Kelleher started getting into craft beer while he was an Ohio State student, but found he could not always afford the higher quality beers on a college salary. That's when he discovered a friend was making his own.

"I thought it would be a really great way to save money and I could try and design the perfect beers for me," he said. "I started doing that and it really took off from there. I was brewing dozens of batches of beer at a time."

His friends also were enjoying the fruits of his labor and recognized his beer-making talent. A

Beers brewed: Year-round: Cranberry Cider, Four North Pale Ale, Buckeye Roots Hefeweizen, Kelleher's Ohio Red, and Bourbon Barrel Stout. Kelleher also was developing other recipes at the time of my visit.

The Pick: The only product I got a chance to sample was the Cranberry Cider, a sweet cider that reminded me of soda.

bunch of them came together and sat him down in a sort of intervention. They suggested that he open his own brewery with them as investors.

Kelleher decided to open a homebrew supply shop, as well, after brewing beer and a cider for a friend's wedding. As he started to make the transition from homebrewer to professional brewer, he realized how much he enjoyed homebrewing and how much he hated shopping for quality ingredients.

Homebrew shops are more costly—sometimes three or four times as much—than shopping on the Internet, Kelleher said. But he hated using the Internet because of the impersonal service and time he had to wait until the ingredients arrived. Not to mention that he didn't like paying shipping costs.

"I realized I wanted to set up a homebrew supply shop like I thought it should be done as a beer brewer myself," he said. "I realized because I buy everything, well for the most part everything, all my hops, all my grains, all of my ingredients, directly from the manufacturers and growers, I could keep the prices about the same as the Internet, if not lower than in a couple of cases, while offering the selection and service that I really liked about brick and mortar stores."

While the shop sells all the beer-making supplies you'd want, including equipment, ingredients, and books, there's one major item missing. Neil House doesn't sell prepackaged kits. Instead, Kelleher develops personalized recipes for his customers.

"What I really like to do is talk to people, because talking with brewers is always fun," he said. "It also kind of gives me a chance to feel out what they're looking for in a beer. If you want a pale ale, what kind of hops do you want? Do you want something real citrusy, real floral? Do you want something real bitter or maybe not bitter at all? Do you want something that has a lot of grainy notes to it? There are so many variables, even within one style of pale ale, that I like to talk to people and help them design the beer they really want to do. I think a lot of people know what they like in beer; they just don't know which ingredients give them that beer."

Kelleher eventually wants to open a brewpub and have his beers distributed throughout Ohio, but said that's a goal for down the road. Instead, he's now focused on growing the brewery and having fun.

"I know that sounds cliché and tacky," he said. "But one of the things that I really enjoy about brewing is trying new things and having fun, and that's where I feel a lot of my inspiration comes from. If we're not having fun here, then I don't know that that inspiration would be there anymore and we'd be making good beer. If we're not making good beer, what are we doing?"

Neil House Brewery

Opened: 2010.
Owner: Patrick Kelleher.
Brewer: Patrick Kelleher.
System: Three half-barrel Brew Magic systems.
Production: 650 barrels.
Distribution: Columbus area.
Hours: Monday and Wednesday, 11 A.M. to 5 P.M.; Friday, 11 A.M. to 6 P.M.
Tours: Upon request.
Take-out beer: Bottles. Kelleher also plans to offer growlers.
Parking: A large parking area is available.
Other area beer sites: See page 84.

Rockmill Brewery

5705 Lithopolis Road, Lancaster, OH 43130
310-755-4097 • www.rockmillbrewery.com

Matthew Barbee wasn't a beer fan—that is, until the day he ordered a Saison Dupont at a restaurant in Venice Beach, California. The Belgian farmhouse ale, which comes in a wine-sized bottle with a cork instead of a cap, intrigued him and opened him to the beer scene. It also got him interested in pairing beer and food, something he had never considered before.

"The server poured it and I was immediately intrigued by the bouquet. 'What is this? Beer can be like this?'" he said. "That's when I became interested in bottle-conditioned beers, where the yeast flavor profile is really prominent. I feel that kind of depth of character is what makes it really great for pairing with foods."

A few years later, Barbee left his job as a talent manager in Los Angeles and moved home to his family's 11-acre property, a former horse farm outside of Lancaster, a community of about thirty-five thousand people south of Columbus. Rockmill Farms couldn't be any more different than Los Angeles. It sits in rolling farmland and at the headwaters of the Hocking River. There isn't a skyscraper in sight. Heck, there's not even a commercial building anywhere nearby.

"I was just looking around at this beautiful farm with the outbuildings not necessarily being utilized and my wheels started turning about what if I were to stay in Ohio," Barbee said. "What would I do that I would be passionate about and would be fulfilling?"

His grandfather had operated a winery and it was Barbee's dream to one day follow in those footsteps. But he didn't want to grow grapes in the Midwest. At the time, he was researching the saison or farmhouse ale style of beer-making—bottle-conditioned beers that are fermented at warmer temperatures and typically bottled in wine-sized bottles. It just so happened that his stepfather, Dennis Smalley, had the water at the farm analyzed and it was almost identical in terms of minerals to Wallonia, a French-speaking portion of Belgium where the saison style originated.

Barbee knew then that he wanted to make farmhouse ales. Remarkably, he wasn't a homebrewer and had never made beer before launching his brewery, which is named after the farm. He is self-taught, having learned the craft through experimentation and reading books as opposed to attending a beer school.

"We chose to take our own path in order to have a true reflection of our DNA and journey in the end product," he said. "I'm really glad we did that because I have a specific learning style and one of my favorite things is exploring a city or exploring a craft. That was a big part of the fun for me, the exploration of it all."

Barbee and Dennis and Judith Smalley converted a section of the former horse stables into the brewhouse. Dennis Smalley, a hydrogeologist by trade, custom built a one-barrel system for the operation, and two former tack rooms were transformed into fermenting rooms where the temperature is kept constantly warm. Meanwhile, Barbee's house, a two-story former barn with an open floor plan, gorgeous wooden floors, and bedroom lofts, has been converted into the tasting room, retail store, music venue, and art gallery.

The stunning property also includes a tiny white chapel, which is popular for weddings, and a large pond. A forty-foot waterfall is within walking distance down the street where a historic six-story gristmill from the 1800s overlooks a large ravine, and people often jump off a cliff into the water pit below. That's where the Native Americans and settlers would come together to trade, Barbee said. They would board horses in the barn that has been converted into Barbee's house.

Beers brewed: Year-round: Witbier, Saison, Dubbel, and Tripel.

The Pick: The Tripel is an organic golden ale that's dry-hopped with coriander and Belgian Saaz hops. At 9 percent alcohol, it also carries a punch, but not in the flavor.

The goal, Barbee said, is to build a monastery-style brewery with a 20-barrel brewhouse on the property. That is down the road, though.

Rockmill sells its four beers in true farmhouse tradition. The beer comes in 750-milliliter bottles with a cork instead of a cap. And all the beers are organic and bottle-conditioned. Because the company is so small—it's just Barbee and his parents—the beer is bottled one at a time and the labels are put on by hand.

The label features a solitary horse in a field and is more a work of art than a traditional beer label. The horse is incorporated because the brewery is located on a former horse farm.

Despite Barbee's enjoyment of farmhouse ales and the Belgian brewing tradition, he is by no means a beer snob. In December 2010, he held a bonfire at the farm and invited people to bring a can of beer. A panel judged the best-tasting beer in a can and the winner received a free four-pack of the Rockmill beers.

In late 2010, the brewery still had a low profile—by choice. The Rockmill website didn't even feature an address, because Barbee didn't want to be inundated with beer travelers. He was more than happy to show people around and set up tastings, but by appointment only.

Rockmill Brewery

Opened: 2010.

Owners: Matthew Barbee and Dennis and Judith Smalley.

Brewer: Matthew Barbee.

System: 1-barrel custom-made system.

Production: 250 barrels.

Distribution: Ohio, but mainly Lancaster and Columbus areas.

Hours: Appointment only.

Tours: Upon request.

Take-out beer: Bottles.

Food: None, but Barbee will hold tastings and pair his beer with cheeses or pastries.

Parking: The parking area also happens to be the family's driveway.

Other area beer sites: See page 84.

Weasel Boy Brewing Company

126 Muskingum Avenue, Suite E, Zanesville, OH 43701
740-455-3767 • www.weaselboybrewing.com

Inspiration struck Jay and Lori Wince while they visited small breweries in Colorado. The couple discovered open and inviting breweries that felt more like intimate coffeehouses. They also encountered places where the brewhouse was out in the open and not behind glass or hidden away from customers.

So when they opened the Weasel Boy Brewing Company in Zanesville in 2007, they created that atmosphere in their brewpub. The brewing equipment is up front and customers have to walk past the brewhouse to get to the bar area. There's also nothing separating customers from the brewing equipment, except for a yellow nylon rope.

As for the seating, it's just like a coffeehouse—small tables and an area filled with a couch, recliner, and chairs that you'd find in your den at home. The Winces also placed magazines, books, and games there. Beer memorabilia, including posters and photos, hang on the walls.

"We thought it was very, very important for the consumer to be right next to the equipment with no barriers," said Jay Wince, who also works full time as a production supervisor at a wholesale bakery. "We felt it gave them a sense of ownership . . . because that's the way we felt when we walked into those places. And we wanted more of a café or coffee shop feel. We wanted people to feel at home so they could sit down and relax in an easy chair and have a beer and read a magazine or converse with friends."

The brewpub is also missing an amenity found in nearly every restaurant and bar. There are no televisions.

"Most of the people who come in probably haven't been in many places that don't have a television in it if it's a restaurant or bar," Jay Wince said. "They find themselves enjoying it much more than maybe they would if there was a television in

Beers brewed: Year-round beers: Plaid Ferret Scottish, Ornery Otter Blonde, White Weasel Wheat, Dancing Ferret IPA, River Mink Mild Brown, and Brown Stoat Stout.

The Pick: When a brewery offers a Great American Beer Festival medalwinner, how could you not pick that? The Anastasia Russian Imperial Stout is a sweet-tasting, dark-as-midnight beer.

the corner, because they come in and interact with their friends or other customers. We've seen a lot of relationships spring up here. People shaking hands and getting to know each other. We wanted it to be a very social place where people interacted and didn't get glued to the television."

Weasel Boy is in a former industrial building that backs up to the Muskingum River. The Winces put a small patio on the back of the brewpub so customers can watch the river meander by. Hop vines grow up a trellis there. The long brick building, built in 1935 and later added onto, once housed the Zanesville Mold Company, which made glass molds. Today, it's an eclectic mix of businesses and residences. The building has an art studio, adult day care, condos, and of course, the brewery.

The brewery is located just outside downtown and down the road from the Zanesville Y bridge, which is listed in the National Register of Historic Places. The bridge, as you might guess, is Y-shaped and spans the confluence of the Muskingum and Licking Rivers.

When the Winces were looking to name their brewery, they thought about the Y-Bridge Brewery. But they opted for Weasel Boy because of their love of ferrets. They got a ferret, a member of the weasel family, before they got married and twenty years later had four of them. A friend used to ask how the "Weasel Boy" was doing and they figured why not name their business that.

The brewery logo is a cartoon weasel, with its long tongue hanging out, looking over a bottle cap. Each Weasel Boy beer comes with a weasel-inspired name. Among them are Plaid Ferret Scottish, Ornery Otter Blonde, and River Mink Mild Brown. Jay likes to keep eight to ten beers on tap and make seasonal and rotating beers, so that's plenty of weasel-related names.

"I do a lot of research," he said. "I'm up to twenty beer names and eighteen are weasels. I think we can never run out of names. We've even done a couple in foreign languages."

One of the beers that doesn't have a weasel name, Anastasia Russian Imperial Stout, won a bronze medal at the Great American Beer Festival in 2010. Jay wasn't sure whether the medal, which hangs behind the bar, will help with sales, but said it was satisfying to be recognized in such a difficult category.

Lori Wince, a reporter for a chain of weekly newspapers in the Columbus area, helps brew. Jay compared brewing to cooking.

"It's kind of like being a great chef," he said. "Anybody can read a recipe, but there are only certain chefs out there really who can make the plate talk to you."

So what are they trying to make the plate say?

"A lot of breweries are trying to beat people over the head with huge beers and almost over-the-top flavors," Jay said. "We're trying to create balance. We want something that if someone doesn't drink stout, they can go, 'Oh that's not too bad.' As opposed to, 'Wow, that's really roasty or dry.' We're trying to convey to our customers the broad palette of flavors that are available in beer. Craft brewers are trying to relay the message that beer is literally hundreds of different flavors from crisp and refreshing to heavy and almost dessert-like. We're just trying to preach the broad range of beer and we're trying to come across in our little corner of that with balance and drinkability."

Weasel Boy Brewing Company

Opened: 2007.

Owners: Jay and Lori Wince.

Brewers: Jay and Lori Wince.

System: CDC seven-barrel system.

Production: 400 barrels.

Distribution: At the brewpub and at some select restaurants and bars in Central and Southeast Ohio.

Hours: Tuesday through Friday, 4 P.M. to midnight; Saturday, 3 P.M. to midnight.

Tours: Upon request.

Take-out beer: Growlers.

Food: The menu is limited to one item: pizza.

Extras: There's live entertainment on Saturdays and sometimes Fridays.

Parking: On-street parking and a lot across from the brewery.

Other area beer sites: See page 84.

Festivals

Ohio has plenty of beer festivals, many focused on beer made in the state. Let's face it, festivals are the best way to sample different brands and styles and figure out which ones suit your personal taste. There's nothing worse than buying a six-pack, bringing it home, and then realizing you don't like it. If that happens, you either end up dumping it down the drain or pawning it off on your friends.

Festivals also are a tremendous opportunity to chat with professional brewers and rub elbows with other knowledgeable beer drinkers. I'll never forget my first—and so far only—visit to the Great American Beer Festival in Denver in 2003. I thought I had died and gone to heaven given the nearly endless number of booths featuring brewery after brewery. I eagerly ran up to taste beer I had only read about in books, magazines, or online.

While there, I also got a chance to talk with Garrett Oliver of Brooklyn Brewery and other brewers who were serving their beer to me. Where else would you get an opportunity like that? You're certainly not going to go to a shoe store and have Phil Knight put a pair of Nikes on your feet.

Ohio has many talented brewers who always are willing to chat about their beer. They know that an educated beer drinker is more likely to try their beer.

A word of warning about beer festivals, though: You have to be very careful, because three or four ounces of beer can catch up to you pretty quick, especially if you're having sample after sample. Make sure you get a designated driver or stay nearby in a hotel so you don't have to drive.

If you're looking for a great source to identify beer festivals near and far, check out www.beerfestivals.org. The website provides a wonderful breakdown of beer festivals around the world. Here's a rundown of some of the larger beer festivals in Ohio.

January

- Columbus Winter Beerfest (www.columbusbeerfest.org). The two-day event is held at the Greater Columbus Convention Center, 400 N. High Street, Columbus.

February

- AleFest Columbus (www.alefest.com/columbus.htm). The festival is held at the Aladdin Shrine Center, 3850 Stelzer Road, Columbus. In addition to the tasting, there is live entertainment and a silent auction featuring beer memorabilia.
- Cincy Winter Beerfest (www.cincybeerfest.com). This two-day event takes place in downtown Cincinnati at the Duke Energy Convention Center. Proceeds benefit the Big Joe Duskin Music Education Foundation.
- Winter Warmer Festival. The event is held in Cleveland and sponsored by the Ohio Craft Brewers Association. It used to be held at the Rock Bottom Brewery restaurant in the Flats, but was looking for a new home after Rock Bottom closed.

March

- Glass City Beer Fest (www.glasscitybeerfest.com). The event is held at the Erie Street Market, 237 S. Erie Street, Toledo. One hundred percent of the proceeds benefit nonprofit organizations.
- AleFeast Dayton (www.alefest.com/alefeast_dayton.htm). The first event in Dayton, which pairs fine food and craft beer, is held at the Dayton Masonic Center, 525 W. Riverview Avenue, Dayton.

April

- The Big Tap In (www.bigtapin.com). The event is held at the Shepherd Event Center, 7469 South Avenue, Boardman.

July

- Ohio Brew Week (www.ohiobrewweek.com). That's not a mistake. It's a brew *week*. Not a day. Not two days. But a week! The event is held every year in Athens. Brew Week, first started in 2006, features beer pairing dinners, talks by well-known folks in the industry, special releases, musical events, homebrew demonstrations, cooking competitions, and of course, the opportunity to try nearly every beer made in the state. Since the weeklong festival is so big, about thirty bars and restaurants throughout Athens take part.

August

- AleFest Dayton (www.alefest.com/dayton.htm). The second event in Dayton is held in Carillon Historical Park, 1000 Carillon Boulevard, Dayton.
- Blues & Brews. For years, this festival was held on the picturesque grounds of Stan Hywet Hall & Gardens in Akron. In 2011, the event moved to Lock 3, an urban park in downtown Akron.

September

- Cleveland Labor Day Oktoberfest (www.clevelandoktoberfest .com). This four-day event is held at the Berea Fairgrounds, 164 Eastland Road, Berea.
- Cincinnati Beer Fest (www.myfountainsquare.com/beerfest). The three-day event is held on Fountain Square in downtown Cincinnati.

October

- Miami Valley Beer Fest (www.mvbeerfest.org). The event is held at the Montgomery County Fairgrounds, 1043 S. Main Street, Dayton.
- Cleveland Beer Week (www.clevelandbeerweek.org). The eight-day event held in Cleveland is similar to Ohio Brew Week and features a beer tasting, beer pairing dinners, talks with big names in the industry, and a homebrew competition at various locations throughout the city.

Southern Ohio

Northern Ohio may have miles and miles of coastline along Lake Erie, But Southern Ohio has miles and miles of shoreline along the Ohio River. The river stretches from the far southwestern corner of the Buckeye State all the way over to East Liverpool in eastern Ohio.

It forms the state's southern border with Kentucky and West Virginia, snaking past communities like Cincinnati, Portsmouth, Ironton, Gallipolis, and Marietta. Southern Ohio really is two distinct regions. There's the Cincinnati area. Then, there's Appalachia, a poor and struggling region dominated by farms, forests, and small towns that are past their glory days.

Ideally, this area would be broken into two sections for this book, but there aren't enough breweries in the southeastern portion of the state to justify its own chapter. So, although it's more than a three-hour ride from Marietta to Cincinnati along back roads and minor highways, I'm lumping the entire Ohio River region into one chapter.

Cincinnati is the cultural center of not only southwestern Ohio, but also northern Kentucky and southeastern Indiana. With more than 2.1 million people in a region that extends beyond Ohio, the Cincinnati metropolitan area is the largest in the state. The community has a major Germanic influence when it comes to beer, and the region is still discovering craft brewers.

Portsmouth, the home to the Portsmouth Brewing Company, is the state's second-largest city along the Ohio River. And that's not saying much considering there are only about twenty thousand people living there. The community is probably best known for the ***Portsmouth Floodwall Murals*** (www.portsmouthohiomurals.com), giant twenty-foot tall paintings that stretch for more than two thousand feet. They serve as a major tourist attraction. In the early 1990s, artist Robert Dafford was commissioned to depict the history of the community on a twenty-foot gray floodwall that was built after a devastating flood in 1937.

Marietta is the other major town along the river with a brewpub, the Marietta Brewing Company. The picturesque river town and home to Marietta College was the first permanent settlement in the Northwest Territory back in 1788.

Dayton isn't on the Ohio River, but it's south of Columbus, so I'm going to throw it in this section. The city, where aviation pioneers Orville and Wilbur Wright grew up, is home to about 160,000 people. Overall, about 840,000 folks live in the metro region. Given the size of the community, it's disappointing and strange that there were no breweries operating in Dayton when I wrote this book in late 2010. Toxic Brew Company had plans to open in the city in 2012.

"Every brewery that opened in Dayton has had poor management or too much management," said Casey McAdams, a homebrewer and webmaster for Belmont Party Supply. "The community would support it as long as the beer is good."

McAdams should know. **Belmont Party Supply** (2621 S. Smithville Road, Dayton, 937-252-4724, www.schwartzbeer.com) has an amazing selection of more than two thousand beers and has been ranked as one of the best beer stores in the country by Ratebeer.com. "The community support is there," McAdams said.

Here's a look at some other beer-related options in Southern Ohio.

- **BJ's Restaurant & Brewhouse** (11700 Princeton Pike, Cincinnati, 513-671-1805, www.bjsbrewhouse.com) is part of a corporate chain based in Huntington Beach, California. BJ's offers plenty of house beers, including several that have won medals at the Great American Beer Festival, but the Cincinnati location doesn't actually brew beer on the premises and instead gets its BJ's beers delivered. (See the "A Word about . . . Other 'Breweries'" on page 141 for more about BJ's, which also has a location in Columbus.)

- **Jungle Jim's International Market** (5440 Dixie Highway, Fairfield, 513-674-6000, www.junglejims.com) describes itself as "not just a store; we're a destination." The "destination" carries about twelve hundred different beers and holds monthly beer tastings. The store is 285,000 square feet and even has a reconditioned monorail from Kings Island operating outside. The front entrance features giant animal statues and a waterfall.

- **Lackman Bar** (1237 Vine Street, Cincinnati, 513-381-3584, www .lackmanbar.com) is inside a turn-of-the-century building constructed by Herman Lackman, founder of the Lackman Brewing Company. The bar features about sixty beers on tap and in bottles.

- **Teller's of Hyde Park** (2710 Erie Avenue, Cincinnati, 513-321-4721, www.tellersofhydepark.com) is an upscale restaurant featuring more than thirty beers on tap and another fifty in bottles. The menu ranges from shrimp pizza to salmon to eggplant cannelloni.

- **The Party Source** (95 Riviera Drive, Bellevue, Kentucky, 859-291-4007, www.thepartysource.com) isn't actually in Cincinnati, or Ohio, but it's just across the Ohio River. The store has a massive selection of beers and kegs, but what's more impressive is that the store sells growlers and offers regular special beer tastings. Mt. Carmel Brewing Company also has made some special small batches exclusively for the Party Source under the name Quaff Bros.

There are several other attractions to visit while you're in the area.

- **Kings Island** (Kings Island Drive, Mason, 513-754-5700, www.visitkingsisland.com) has more than eighty rides, shows, and attractions. It's just north of Cincinnati and is visible from Interstate 71. About three million people a year visit the amusement park, which opened in 1972. It features the longest wooden roller coaster in the world, The Beast, and a 15-acre waterpark called Boomerang Bay. The park is owned by Cedar Fair Entertainment, the same firm that operates Cedar Point in Sandusky.

- **American Sign Museum** (2515 Essex Place, Cincinnati, 513-258-4020, www.signmuseum.net) is an offbeat attraction. The nonprofit museum was founded by Tod Swormstedt, former editor and publisher of *Signs of the Times* magazine. The museum has more than twenty-eight hundred items, including signs, sign-making equipment, and artwork. The signs range from painted to neon.

- **Cincinnati Zoo and Botanical Garden** (3400 Vine Street, Cincinnati, 513-281-4700, www.cincinnatizoo.org) consistently is ranked as one of the best zoos in the nation. It features more than five hundred animals and three thousand plants. More than one million people a year visit the zoo.

- **The National Underground Railroad Freedom Center** (50 E. Freedom Way, Cincinnati, 513-333-7500, www.freedomcenter.org) offers exhibits in a museum setting. Ohio played an important role in the Underground Railroad helping runaway slaves, and there are several other historic spots to visit in Marietta (www .mariettaohio.org/undergroundrailroad).

- **National Aviation Hall of Fame** (1100 Spaatz Street, Dayton, 888-383-1903, www.nationalaviation.org). Anyone interested in flying will be interested in visiting Wright-Patterson Air Force Base in Dayton. It's home to the National Aviation Hall of Fame, which recognizes the country's air and space pioneers. The nonprofit organization, founded in 1962, has a 17,000-square-foot Learning Center with interactive exhibits. Among the inductees are Ohio natives Orville and Wilbur Wright.

- **The National Museum of the U.S. Air Force** (1100 Spaatz Street, Dayton, 937-255-3286, www.nationalmuseum.af.mil) also can be found on the base and features galleries and exhibits about the Air Force.

Christian Moerlein Brewing Company

Quite Simply a Better Beer

CHRISTIAN MOERLEIN BREWING COMPANY

1621 Moore Street, Cincinnati, OH 45202
www.christianmoerlein.com

Greg Hardman can still recall the thrill it was to get an invitation to tour the Hudepohl brewery in Cincinnati in the mid-1980s. At the time, he was a young beer distributor in Athens, selling a ton of the brewery's Burger brand in the college town.

But as the tour progressed, his excitement faded. The tour guide pointed to the bottling line and mentioned that those were some of the last bottles being made by the brewery, which was merging with the Schoenling Brewing Company. A few years later, he saw the Hudepohl-Schoenling distributorship, the last brewery-owned distributor in Ohio at the time, sold to a local beer distributor who represented mostly national brands, effectively ending Cincinnati's brewery-owned distribution system. He also watched as the famous Cincinnati brands Christian Moerlein, Hudepohl, Burger, and Little Kings languished and the city's once-proud brewing heritage faded.

"I swore if I was ever in a position, I would right that wrong," Hardman said.

Today, he's doing just that. Hardman, a former president and chief executive officer of Warsteiner Brauerie, KG North American Operations, began buying up the old Cincinnati brands in 2004 and relaunching them with vigor. His original plan was to focus on the higher-end craft Christian Moerlein brand, but he was inundated with requests from the community to bring back Hudepohl, Little Kings, Burger, and other brands.

Hardman has taken some criticism for not brewing any of the beer in Cincinnati, but he dismissed that, noting that both Boston Beer Company and Brooklyn Brewery—now well-respected brands—started by renting brewery space from other brewers before buying their own facilities. He is merely following their model.

As of this writing, Hardman's brands are being made at his new brewing facility in the Over-the-Rhine Brewery District in Cincinnati, as well as at breweries in La Crosse, Wisconsin, and Wilkes-Barre and Latrobe, Pennsylvania. The beer is available in bottles and cans throughout Greater Cincinnati and some, like Little Kings Cream Ale, can be found in many states. Hardman purchased a former Husman's potato chip factory—the onetime Kauffman Brewery—to house his production brewery, which opened in December 2010 and made the first Christian Moerlein in Over-the-Rhine since the start of Prohibition in 1919.

The beer brewed was a tribute to the 150th anniversary of Cincinnati's oldest continuous operating saloon, Arnold's Bar and Grill. Arnold's 1861 Porter was unveiled at the stroke of midnight on January 1, 2011.

Also in 2011, Hardman planned to open the Moerlein Lager House, a 22,500-square-foot brewpub along the Ohio River and right next to Great American Ball Park, home of the Cincinnati Reds.

"We're all about reviving Cincinnati's great brewing history," said Hardman, a talkative and friendly guy.

The Over-the-Rhine neighborhood, just a short distance from the heart of downtown, is a rough, rundown area filled with two- and three-story row buildings built in the late 1800s and early 1900s. Many are Italianate and some are Greek Revival style, likely gorgeous in their heyday. The neighborhood was home to all of Cincinnati's major breweries and many of those buildings are still standing.

Hardman made a remarkable discovery after buying the former potato chip factory. About thirty feet below his production brewery

Beers brewed: Year-round: Christian Moerlein Lager House Helles, Christian Moerlein OTR Over-the-Rhine Ale, Christian Moerlein Barbarossa Double Dark, Christian Moerlein Northern Liberties IPA, Christian Moerlein Seven Weiss, Hudy Delight, Hudy 14-K, Hudepohl Amber Lager, Burger Classic, Burger Light, and Little Kings Cream Ale. The Christian Moerlein and Hudepohl lineups also feature seasonal beers.

The Pick: The Christian Moerlein OTR Over-the-Rhine Ale is a well-balanced American pale ale that hits you with both big hops and bigger malt character, with a caramel finish. It also has a lasting flavor.

are lagering cellars once used by the Kauffman Brewery. The expansive cellars are well preserved, with hand-built stone walls and high-arching ceilings. They were used to keep beer cool during the lagering process, but after modern refrigeration was invented, the cellars were abandoned and sealed off. Hardman wasn't even aware they existed when he bought the building.

The Over-the-Rhine Brewery District, a community urban redevelopment group, constructed a wooden staircase down to the cellars to provide tours. The neighborhood is filled with cellars, some of them still undiscovered, because there were so many breweries there, said Steven Hampton, an architect and executive director of the district. At the time of my visit, Hardman served as president of the group.

The production brewery, located on Moore Street, is 125,000 square feet, so the brewing operation can start out small and grow there, Hardman said. He plans to start off brewing the Christian Moerlein brands and Hudepohl Amber Lager at the site. He also wants to open a taproom where people can sample all the Cincinnati brands.

Meanwhile, the brewpub, scheduled to open in late 2011, will be in a contemporary building with huge windows overlooking the Ohio River and a giant lawn. It also will feature two large beer gardens and two eateries, one focusing on traditional brewpub fare and the other focusing on hand-carved meats, such as prime rib, pork, and turkey. All of the Christian Moerlein brands will be available at the bars inside. Hardman also planned to serve guest beers.

Each room at the Moerlein Lager House will be named after a different Cincinnati brewery. The brewpub also will have a special room dedicated to the city's former beer barons, Christian Moerlein chief among them. Each will receive a plaque and a storyboard honoring his contribution. Hardman also was trying to get some bricks from every brewery in the city to install in a special brick wall inside the brewpub.

He wants to tie the new brewpub to the Over-the-Rhine neighborhood, so there will be a shuttle available to take people on a historical tour of the old brewery district and to the Christian Moerlein production brewery.

"It's been my lifelong dream and work to bring back Cincinnati's grand brewing traditions," said Hardman, the city's newest beer baron. "My motto is 'Go big or go home.' I've never been short on the vision for going big and have been successful in doing so. You know, I didn't create Cincinnati's brewing history, but I'm going to celebrate it. I felt I was the only guy who had the knowledge, skill-set, and the resources to pull all of this off, and Cincinnati is going to celebrate its grand brewing heritage in a way that no other city in America has done so far."

Christian Moerlein Brewing Company

Opened: 2004. Christian Moerlein opened a production brewery in December 2010 and a brewpub is planned to open 2011.

Owner: Greg Hardman.

Brewer: Mike Carver.

Production: 50,000 barrels.

Distribution: Christian Moerlein and Hudepohl brands are available only in the Greater Cincinnati area. Little Kings Cream Ale is in thirty-nine states. The Burger brand is available in thirteen states.

Hours: Visit the website for hours.

Take-out beer: Planned for the Moerlein Lager House.

Tours: Hardman planned to offer tours as soon as the production brewery is open.

Food: The Moerlein Lager House will feature two restaurants. One will have a traditional brewpub menu, while the other will focus on rotisserie hand-carved meats.

Parking: On-street and in a small lot across from the production facility. There is an underground parking deck and on-street parking at the brewpub.

Other area beer sites: See page 114.

Jackie O's Pub and Brewery

24 W. Union Street, Athens, OH 45701
740-592-9686 • www.jackieos.com

Brewer Brad Clark is a mad scientist when it comes to making beer. Pecans? Sure. Walnuts? Why not. Bacon? Toss some of that in. Age a beer with real cherries in a cabernet barrel? Let's give it a try.

Clark's penchant for experimentation, his desire to have plenty of house beers on tap, and the overall quality of his beer have earned rave reviews from critics around the world. Not bad for a small brewpub in the middle of nowhere that offers 22-ounce bottles on special occasions.

"We're this little place doing big things," owner Art Oestrike said. "It's pretty badass to hear those things."

Jackie O's is located in Athens, a city along the Hocking River in southeastern Ohio. Athens is home to Ohio University, including its twenty-one thousand students, and when it comes to beer, the town is known more for its love of quantity than quality. Its annual Halloween celebration is legendary, with tens of thousands of costumed and tipsy people wandering the downtown.

The brewery dates to 1996, when the bar, then known as O'Hooleys Pub, added the brewhouse. O'Hooleys went out of business and Oestrike bought the place in December 2005.

He kept the name, at least in the beginning, but around the same time, his mother was diagnosed with cancer and passed away. He decided to rename the bar Jackie O's in her honor. Not many people know that story. There are photos of John F. Kennedy on the wall and visitors just assume it was named after Jackie Onassis.

Clark was a student at Ohio University majoring in creative writing and working the door at O'Hooleys when the bar went out of business. He had struck up a friendship with Oestrike, who also owns the Bagel Street Deli downtown and teaches some English as a second language courses at the university. Oestrike asked Clark to stay on and serve as his brewer.

Clark, a homebrewer, headed off to the Siebel Institute of Technology in Chicago to learn the professional side of the craft and took over the brewing duties in 2006.

"Before we were here, it was hard to find American craft beers here," Clark said about the local beer selection. "There was definitely nothing from Europe really. And it's come a long way now. Sometimes we'll have tons of craft beers. Some German lagers. Some Baltic porters. And a beer from Japan and some Belgian abbey stuff all on draft at once. And people seem to really like that."

He doesn't bother worrying about college kids who may be more into Miller Lite or Natural Light. "We've got a real good customer base of grad students, professors, a lot of locals. And then we have a lot of students, as well. Sometimes it's really surprising. You'll come in and there's a bunch of young kids sitting at a table and they've all got snifters with a barrel-aged imperial stout."

Jackie O's, which is split into two separate buildings, sits in the shadow of Ohio University on West Union Street. The original building is tiny and old, dating back to 1890. It is a quintessential, well-worn, college-looking bar—other than the brewhouse and fermenters.

The brewhouse is behind a small, circular bar with handcrafted, wooden tap handles, while the fermenters are up front. There are no

Beers brewed: Year-round: Firefly Amber, Ohio Pale Ale, Mystic Mama IPA, Drawn & Portered, Chomolungma Organic Honey Nut Brown, and Razz Wheat. The brewpub also offers a slew of seasonal and rotating beers.

The Pick: The barrel-aged Dark Apparition is amazing. It's a thick Russian imperial stout that's so warming going down, but doesn't have the overpowering bourbon flavor as many others.

pipes to move the liquid from one side of the bar to the other. Instead, Clark has to schlep a hose across the length of the bar floor, something that's sometimes done while there are customers milling about. It's a wonder the beer is so tasty given that setup.

The real gem is in the cellar, which is crammed with barrels containing Clark's latest experiments. There are no televisions in the original bar, but there is a stage along one side of the wall that folds down for live music, kind of like a hide-a-bed that gets pulled out whenever needed.

A large concrete patio in the back connects the brewhouse bar to the other Jackie O's, a larger, more open bar that serves food and is known as The Public House. There are televisions here and the bar is much larger. The tables are made out of former bourbon barrels.

Jackie O's offers plenty of house beers, around ten or eleven, and many guest beers. And they keep rotating. Clark estimates that he brews about fifty different beers a year. When it comes to naming the beer, Clark takes inspiration from Frank Zappa. He's a Zappa fan who often slips in Zappa references.

For example, the Oil of Aphrodite, a thick imperial stout made with four chocolate malts, locally harvested black walnuts, and Belgian dark syrup, was pulled from the song "Cozmik Debris."

There are two exceptional times to visit Jackie O's. The bar serves as the unofficial home for Ohio Brew Week, a weeklong celebration of craft beer made in the state. The event is held annually in July in Athens. Then there's the bar's anniversary party in December, when Jackie O's puts thirty-eight of its own beers on draft at a single time. People have come from as far as Alabama and Florida.

"It's so cool," Oestrike said about the response.

Jackie O's Pub and Brewery

Opened: 2006.

Owner: Art Oestrike.

Brewer: Brad Clark.

System: 7-barrel DME Brewing Services.

Production: 850 barrels.

Distribution: At the brewpub and occasionally at some bars and restaurants in Columbus.

Hours: The Public House is open Monday through Friday, 11:30 A.M. to 2 A.M.; and Saturday and Sunday, 9 A.M. to 2 A.M. The brewery is open Tuesday through Saturday, 4:30 P.M. to 2 A.M.

Tours: Upon request.

Take-out beer: Growlers. There also are occasional special bottle releases.

Food: The menu is high-end pub food with a local twist. The menu ranges from burgers to pizzas made with spent grains from the brewing process.

Extras: The bar offers live entertainment and holds special beer festivals throughout the year.

Parking: On-street parking.

Other area beer sites: See page 114.

Listermann Brewing Company

1621 Dana Avenue, Cincinnati, OH 45207
513-731-1130 • www.listermann.com

Dan Listermann blurted out two short words when asked to describe his brewery: "Very small." Then he laughed. He's not kidding.

Listermann Brewing, which sells its beer on the premises in 22-ounce bottles, produced only thirty barrels in 2008. For comparison, fellow Cincinnati beer-maker Rivertown Brewing made fifteen hundred barrels in its first year and it's considered small.

First and foremost, Listermann is a homebrew shop rather than a full-fledged commercial brewery. The business, housed in a one-story redbrick and concrete-block building, sells all the ingredients and equipment needed to make beer. Need hops? He's got them. Need a kit? He's got them. Need grain? It's there.

The shop is located in the city's working-class Evanston neighborhood, perhaps best known as the birthplace of Doris Day. It's also on the doorstep of Xavier University, a Jesuit Catholic university with about seven thousand students and a perennial NCAA basketball powerhouse.

Dan Listermann's love affair with beer-making started out with a bang—and not the good kind. He calls his first experiences the "1973 disasters." At the time, he was in college at Miami University in Oxford, Ohio, when he decided to make a batch of beer from a crude kit that he bought at a drugstore.

"It was a pound of malt, an ounce of hops and instructions," he said. "You were supposed to boil them all together with 5 pounds of sugar, cool it down, and put it in a brand-new garbage can with a package of Fleishmann's yeast."

Most of the bottles foamed over or exploded. He made a few batches after that, and for some reason they got increasingly worse. So he gave up. It wasn't until the late 1980s when he ventured into brewing again, albeit skeptically. A friend asked him to help make some beer and it turned out pretty good.

"I really haven't looked back," said Listermann, an engineer by trade.

As he got more into the homebrewing hobby, he realized he was unhappy with bottle fillers at the time. So he invented his own and started up Listermann Manufacturing Company, a business in his basement. Then he figured as long as he was selling bottle fillers, why not open up a homebrew shop. In 1995, he started one of the first retail homebrew shops in Cincinnati.

Beers brewed: Year-round beers: Wild Mild, Friar Bacon Smoke Bock Beer, Beef Trust Stout, No. 42 Cream Ale, Enter the Beagle IPA, and 186,000 MPS Malt Liquor. Other styles also are made throughout the year.

The Pick: The Friar Bacon Smoked Bock is worth a try. But be careful. People either love smoke beer or hate it. And the Friar Bacon is not misnamed. There's an overwhelming bacon flavor to it.

It was always his dream to brew commercially, but it wasn't until 2008 when he started selling what he made as Listermann Brewing Company beer. He had bought a small system from a brewery that went out of business in Port Clinton, Ohio.

The commercial brewing hasn't been an economic success and Listermann has questioned whether it's worth the time and effort. He also learned something about himself. While he loves brewing beer, he's not a salesman.

"I don't sell beer," he said. "My personality isn't oriented that way. I have a hard time taking it places and selling it. I expect people to come running to my doorstep."

That explains why the beer is available only at his homebrew shop, as opposed to sitting on retail store shelves or at bars and restaurants, and why many people don't even know Listermann is a state-licensed brewery.

Listermann plans to open a tasting room in the front portion of the shop, hoping that draws more people, including those from the expanding Xavier campus, and boosts sales.

He makes an interesting range of bottle-conditioned beers in his messy brewhouse, which is located in a back room. The labels feature the slogan, "It's Too Tasty!" The brewery offers niche styles that you don't often see from small craft brewers, including a smoke beer, cream ale, and malt liquor. Listermann brews what he likes. His favorite style is rauchbier, or smoke beer, and his eyes light up when talking about it.

"I've found the majority [of beer drinkers] seem to like it," he said. "It's very polarizing. You either love it or hate it. But far more people seem to like it than hate it."

He doesn't see anything special, however, about making India pale ales, which he enjoys drinking, and his wicked sense of humor comes through when talking about IPAs.

"Any fool can make that beer," he laughed. "You just throw a lot of hops in it."

Listermann Brewing Company

Opened: 2008.

Owner: Dan Listermann.

Brewer: Dan Listermann.

System: A 2-barrel mix-and-match system.

Production: 30 barrels.

Distribution: The Listermann retail shop.

Hours: Monday through Saturday, 10 A.M. to 6 P.M.

Tours: Any time during regular business hours.

Take-out: 22-ounce bottles. Listermann plans to open a tasting room.

Food: None, but the brewery plans to offer snacks when the tasting room opens.

Parking: A 100-space lot is located across the street.

Other area beer sites: See page 114.

Marietta Brewing Company

MARIETTA BREWING COMPANY

167 Front Street, Marietta, OH 45750
740-373-3195 • www.mbcpub.com

When brewer Mike Arnold says he has deep roots in Marietta, he's not kidding. His mother and father grew up in nearby small towns, and he and his sister were raised in the city.

"My family has lived here for several years and my family tree is quite large with cousins and all," he said. "My great-grandfather built cedar chests to earn money during the Depression from local cedar trees and my other grandfather was a coal miner. The heritage that my family has here really means a lot to me and it is a big part of my brewing."

Arnold took over as head brewer in late 2010, succeeding longtime brewer Kelly Sauber, who had been at Marietta Brewing Company since 1998. He described himself as an easygoing guy who loves to talk with people about the brewing process.

"Since I am from Marietta, it makes it more special to me that I can be the brewer in our local brewery and make beer for the people of this city and surrounding areas," he said.

Marietta, which has a population of less than fifteen thousand people, sits at the confluence of the Muskingum and Ohio Rivers in southeastern Ohio. It was the first permanent settlement in the Northwest Territory in 1788 and the community has a strong brewing heritage. At one point, there were thirteen breweries operating in the Marietta area, including a Marietta Brewing Company.

Today, it's an industrial town fueled by chemical and power plants along the Ohio River, but it's also home to Marietta College and Washington State Community College. The Marietta Washington County Convention & Visitors Bureau describes the community as a "picturesque riverboat town, where the past peacefully resides with the present."

The brewpub itself is set in a long and narrow, 21-by-175-foot brick building downtown. It's a row building and yet it's not. The site originally was an alley, and interestingly Marietta Brewing doesn't own the brick walls on either side, just the space between and the high ceiling.

The brewpub has a modern restaurant feel, with the exposed heating and ventilation systems, exposed brick walls, and wooden bar. There also are old-fashioned advertising logos painted on the walls. The brewhouse is in a glass-enclosed area in the front of the restaurant for all to see as they walk in, but because space is at a premium, the fermenters are in a loft above. That means Arnold has to climb a steep metal ladder many times each day. Sometimes customers don't even notice him up there since it's so high above them.

"Marietta Brewing Company is a down-to-earth place," Arnold said. "It is a place where you can hang out, enjoy good food and good beer

Beers brewed: Year-round: Golden Otter, McLaren's Scotch Ale, Marietta Pale Ale, Brick Street Red Ale, and Raspberry Wheat. The brewery also has rotating and seasonal beers.

The Pick: The McLaren's Scotch Ale is unusual to say the least. The beer is unfiltered, so it's cloudy; it's strange to see a darker beer with a haze. Arnold also uses 20 to 25 pounds of peat malt and a little roasted barley in each batch, giving the beer a real smoky flavor.

on a weekday or weekend. There is live music on the weekends always and there are other things to do in the brewery from playing pool to playing a few arcade games."

As for the beer itself, Arnold said he enjoys brewing different styles and his goal is to have something available to please any beer drinker.

"Heck, I drink about anything," he said. "If it's really unique, the better. It doesn't matter from stouts to porters, India pale ales, scotch ales, the lagers, and so on. I wouldn't say I have a favorite style of brewing, but I like the brewers out there that push the limits of beer."

He's done some of that "bending of the rules," including making a honey ale, with nothing but a little two-row barley and clover honey, and a hickory nut brown ale.

Sauber had created a signature beer for the brewpub, Pawpaw Wheat. The pawpaw is the largest native tree fruit in North America and is sometimes referred to as the poor man's banana. Each September, Ohioans gather to pay homage to the mango-like, seed-filled fruit at the Ohio Pawpaw Festival in nearby Albany. The Ohio Division of Travel & Tourism has called the three-day event one of the state's top fall attractions.

"What makes that beer special to so many people is the unique taste of the citrus and smooth character it has," said Arnold, who collects bottle caps from beers he's tried. He has more than 350.

People also likely enjoy the higher alcohol content—about 8 percent—and the fact that the fruit is locally harvested, he added. He plans on continuing to brew the beer, but likely only as a seasonal offering in the spring.

"I am a brewer for many reasons," Arnold said. "First of all, I love beer. But for the most part, making beer is a trade that not everyone can do. You have to have the love for the flavors, the aromas, and the body of different beers. Making beer makes me happy and when I see a person enjoying one of my beers, I hope I have made that person's day or made them happy at that particular time."

Marietta Brewing Company

Opened: 1997.
Owner: Tony and Dana Styer.
Brewer: Mike Arnold.
System: 7-barrel JV Northwest system.
Production: 500 barrels.
Distribution: At the brewpub and some select off-site accounts in the area.

Hours: Monday through Wednesday, 11 A.M. to 11 P.M.; Thursday, 11 A.M. to 1 A.M.; Friday and Saturday, 11 A.M. to 2 A.M. Closed on Sunday. The kitchen closes earlier.

Tours: Upon request.

Take-out beer: Growlers.

Food: Traditional American pub food that ranges from pizza to Lake Erie perch.

Extras: The brewpub offers live music every Friday and Saturday night. The restaurant also does catering.

Parking: On-street, metered parking.

Other area beer sites: See page 114.

Mt. Carmel Brewing Company

4362 Mt. Carmel-Tobasco Road, Mt. Carmel, OH 45244
513-240-2739 • www.mtcarmelbrewingcompany.com

It's easy to drive past the Mt. Carmel Brewing Company and never know it's there—even if you're looking for it. The brewery is in a century-old, two-story farmhouse in a residential area. It's a white vinyl-sided building with black shutters and a giant front porch. That's not exactly where you would expect to find a craft brewery.

The story of why it's there is an interesting one. Brewery owners Mike and Kathleen Dewey had bought the 2-acre property as an investment with the idea of living there for awhile, eventually buying some land around them and then moving on. At the time, Mike owned a construction company and Kathleen was in real estate.

Mike started brewing in a small barn behind the house as a hobby. He got pretty good at it. As he got better, he built a system in the basement of the house. Mike also was friends with a brewer at the Oldenberg Brewing Company across the Ohio River in Kentucky. The two would brew together and Mike soaked up the commercial aspect of brewing.

"Mike's engineer side kicked in and he just kept making the system better, better, better and better," Kathleen said.

Beers brewed: Year-round: Blonde Ale, Amber Ale, Nut Brown Ale, Stout, and IPA. Mt. Carmel also offers seasonal beers.

The Pick: Everything from Mt. Carmel is solid, but I'm partial to the Nut Brown Ale, which has roasted malts and a hint of maple.

With Mike's brewing skills improving and recognition that there was a lack of craft beer in the Cincinnati market, Kathleen said they concluded: "This is crazy. Let's just get licensed and sell this stuff."

Mt. Carmel was born in 2005. As far as Kathleen knows, Mt. Carmel was the only commercial brewery in the state operating out of a residential property at the time. (The land was rezoned commercial after an expansion and the Deweys moved out.)

Kathleen, who handles the business side of the operation, said her job of selling the beer was easy. The brewery didn't advertise and was not even in the phone book. But people heard about Mt. Carmel and found them.

"Cincinnati was so excited to have a small craft brewer," she said. Oddly enough, Mt. Carmel isn't in Cincinnati or even in Hamilton County. Instead, the brewery is in Clermont County, which calls itself Cincinnati's East Side. And Mt. Carmel is about a half-hour drive from downtown.

In the beginning, the brewery made a name for itself by selling in growlers—not bottles—at grocery stores and other retail outlets.

"People just kept wanting it," Kathleen said. "I can't believe people want the beer and they just kept calling and saying it's really good. And we were adding on styles. It got bigger, bigger, and bigger, and we had to move out. Within about eight months, we had to move out of the brewery in the basement. We could no longer supply enough beer."

The Deweys built an expansion onto the back of the house to handle larger equipment and capacity, but Mike still uses a seven-barrel system, requiring him to brew up to four times a day two or three times a week.

In addition to moving the brewery out of the basement, the Deweys, including their two children, moved out of the farmhouse. Today, a living room is an office. A family room is an office. A kitchen area is the break room. And a former garage and mud room is a small retail shop where framed articles about the brewery hang on the walls and they sell beer, T-shirts, and pint glasses.

In 2009, Mt. Carmel made a radical change—at least for the Deweys. For four years, they had been selling beer to the public only in growlers and to bars and restaurants in kegs. But they decided to scrap the growlers for 12-ounce longneck bottles.

The switch gained them new fans and opened up new markets, but there was a downside. The brewery suddenly couldn't keep up with demand. The Cincinnati media reported how the brewery was struggling with its increased popularity. What did those stories do? Well, of course, it just fueled more demand.

"It almost buried us," Kathleen said.

Mike and another employee were working eighty- and ninety-hour weeks just to keep up. Part of the problem was Mt. Carmel bottled by hand, a tedious process that involves filling each bottle individually. They ended up buying a small bottling system that fills six bottles at a time.

Mt. Carmel survived the rush and continues to grow. The distribution area is now all of Ohio, and a long-term goal is to sell their beer nationwide.

"If people are buying it, sell it," Kathleen said. "But we are very much believers in slow growth. That is why we didn't dump a million dollars into this business out the gate. It was all our own money and slowly building it year after year after year."

The Mt. Carmel philosophy about beer isn't extreme. The Deweys want to make a tasty craft beer that's affordable. Kathleen said the cost for consumers is important and they don't want the beer to be priced high.

"They aren't these crazy extreme beers," she said in describing their styles. "They are good, well-balanced, flavorful, honest, all-natural beers. They are handcrafted and made in very small batches. That's our philosophy."

The brewery did branch out in 2011 by starting a series of bigger beers called "Snapshot." "The idea is that they will never brew it again," Kathleen said. "If, however, the market demands that we brew it again, they may be talked into it."

Mt. Carmel Brewing Company

Opened: 2005.

Owners: Mike and Kathleen Dewey.

Brewer: Mike Dewey.

System: 7-barrel system.

Production: 4,000 barrels.

Distribution: Ohio.

Hours: Monday through Friday, 10 A.M. to 4 P.M.; Saturday, 10 A.M. to 1 P.M.

Tours: Saturday, 10 A.M. to 1 P.M. or by appointment.

Take-out beer: A small retail shop sells bottled beer. There is no sampling on the premises.

Parking: On-site.

Other area beer sites: See page 114.

Portsmouth Brewing Company

224 2nd Street, Portsmouth, OH 45662
740-354-6106

The Portsmouth Brewing Company is in an old, redbrick building—well, actually two buildings—that used to house the original Portsmouth Brewing Company, which dates back to 1843 and was the community's first commercial brewery.

A brick alley used to run between two of the brewery buildings, but along the way the alley was enclosed. That former alley, now called the Brewery Arcade, serves as the entrance to the brewpub. Visitors walk into a building-long atrium. Antiques, such as an old sled and tools, hang on the walls. There's even an old piano up front.

The brewhouse is in the building on the right and is readily visible through glass windows from the atrium. The bar and restaurant are on the left. The bar itself is small and relegated to a corner. Old items, such as snowshoes, golf clubs, and framed letters from the old Portsmouth Brewing, hang on the walls here as well. The brewery makes only draft beer and doesn't bottle. Six house beers are typically on tap, with Portsmouth Pilsner and Red Bird Ale available year-round.

Portsmouth is a small city of about twenty thousand people at the confluence of the Ohio and Scioto Rivers. It's home to Shawnee State University, a small college with about forty-three hundred students.

Just around the corner from the brewpub are the famous Portsmouth Floodwall Murals, a major tourist attraction. A twenty-foot floodwall was built after a devastating flood in 1937 that left one million people homeless and caused more than $500 million in damage along the river from Pittsburgh to Cairo, Illinois.

In the early 1990s, artist Robert Dafford of Lafayette, Louisiana, was commissioned to bring the gray floodwall to life with color and depict the history of Portsmouth over the last two hundred years. The murals range from scenes of Native Americans to a canal boat to Roy Rogers, who was born in Portsmouth. Dafford completed the project in 2002 and the murals are considered the largest work of art done by a single artist, according to the Portsmouth Scioto County Visitor's Bureau.

Beers brewed: Year-round: Portsmouth Pilsner and Red Bird Ale. Rotating and seasonal beers also are available. The brewpub normally has six house beers on tap at all times.

The Pick: The Portsmouth Pilsner is crisp and clean, exactly what you would want out of a lawnmower beer.

Portsmouth Brewing Company

Opened: Not sure, but it got its brewing license from the Ohio Department of Liquor Control in 1997.

Owner: Steven Mault.

Brewers: Tony Thompson and Mark Allen.

System: 10-barrel Saaz system.

Distribution: At the brewpub or at Scioto Ribber, a restaurant in town.

Hours: The summer hours are Monday through Thursday, 11 A.M. to 10 P.M.; Friday and Saturday, 11 A.M. to 11 P.M.; and Sunday, noon to 10 P.M.

Take-out beer: Growlers and kegs.

Food: Ranges from beer-battered chicken wings to pizza to sandwiches.

Parking: On-street parking and a lot across the street.

Other area beer sites: See page 114.

Quarter Barrel Brewery & Pub

107 E. Church Street, Oxford, OH 45056
513-523-2525

Quarter Barrel Brewery & Pub is a bit different from your average brewpub. For starters, there are bookshelves, filled with used books, along two walls. Then, there's the coffee bar in one corner, offering up espresso, set away from the regular bar serving alcoholic drinks.

The large, open brewpub has the feel of an upscale coffeeshop more than a brewery. Owners Brandon Ney, Janet Holmes, and Chris Hensey wanted it that way—with Ney calling the look "upscale eclectic." Quarter Barrel Brewery is located in Oxford, home to Miami University and seventeen thousand students at the main campus.

Wherever there are college students, there are college bars, and those bars are much more interested in quantity than quality. Quarter Barrel provides an oasis of sorts. It's in a large, redbrick building just a block off the main drag, where those college bars proliferate.

When the owners were devising plans for a restaurant, they weren't thinking about becoming a

Beers brewed: Quarter Barrel Brewing has only one beer on tap at any time and that beer is constantly changing with the tastes of the brewer.

The Pick: This is easy. Since there's only one house beer on tap, try that one.

brewpub, but there weren't any reasonably priced liquor licenses available. There's a loophole of sorts in Ohio law that allows businesses to start a brewery and obtain a full liquor license. So that's what they did.

Ney purchased a small and self-contained Newlands System brewhouse and Quarter Barrel Brewery was born. The copper system is on full display behind one section of the bar. The brewhouse is so small—it can produce less than a barrel a batch—that Quarter Barrel offers only one house beer at a time. Because of its size, Ney, who serves as brewer, also doesn't brew the same beer each time, so there's always something different on tap. He anticipated having a few different beers available each month.

To set Quarter Barrel apart from other breweries, Ney also is making cask-conditioned ales, which are served unpasteurized and unfiltered. Because these ales are naturally carbonated and not infused with any gas, they tend to be creamier or, as some might suggest, flatter. Ney is a big supporter of the Campaign for Real Ales movement.

"We're trying to maximize our niche quality by brewing predominately cask-conditioned ales and doing things in a more traditional English way, if not traditional English beer," said Ney, a homebrewer who was managing another Oxford restaurant before opening Quarter Barrel.

Quarter Barrel does offer several craft beers on tap to supplement the beer selection, and there's an emphasis on providing a variety that more discriminating beer drinkers would enjoy. Those included Bell's Two Hearted, Stone Arrogant Bastard, and Mt. Carmel Amber during a visit.

With the coffee, beer, and books, it can be a little difficult to describe Quarter Barrel Brewery. Even Ney struggled a bit, eventually settling on "a less traditional pub focusing on finer aspects of our industry, including coffee, food, wine, and mixed drinks." He noted that it's the type of place where parents get a babysitter to go out. The crowd also varies greatly, he added, from college students looking for better beer to local professionals.

The food is upscale bistro. The owners had planned on using the term "gastropub" in their name, but then figured it wouldn't translate well in southwestern Ohio. Quarter Barrel Brewery offers items such as cracker pizzas, flat iron steak, oven-roasted chicken, and seafood specials.

The books, housed in converted wine cases, are available for people to read and even take home. The owners just ask that you bring and leave two if you plan to take one.

"We're striking the atmosphere chord pretty strong," Ney said.

Quarter Barrel Brewery & Pub

Opened: 2010.

Owners: Brandon Ney, Janet Holmes, and Chris Hensey.

Brewer: Brandon Ney.

System: 1-hecaliter Newlands system.

Production: 45 barrels.

Distribution: At the brewpub only.

Hours: Monday through Saturday, 7 A.M. to 1 A.M. Closed Sunday.

Tours: The system is small and on display, but workers are available to explain the process.

Take-out beer: None.

Food: Upscale bistro, offering sandwiches for lunch and dinner, ranging from steak and seafood to oven-roasted chicken.

Extras: The brewpub also has a coffee bar.

Parking: On-street.

Other area beer sites: See page 114.

Rivertown Brewing Company

607 Shepherd Lane, Unit 6, Lockland, OH 45215
513-827-9280 • www.rivertownbrewery.com

Despite similar backgrounds, Rivertown Brewing owners Jason Roeper and Randy Schiltz didn't really know each other before founding their brewery in late 2009. Both men were in the auto industry. Roeper was in finance with Ford. Schiltz was a manufacturing specialist with Toyota.

Both men were also homebrewers in the same brew club, the Bloatarian Brewing League. Both had aspirations to open a brewpub. And both came to realize they couldn't go it alone. That's when fellow homebrew club members got them together and Rivertown was born.

They ended up scaling back plans for a brewpub after banks and the Small Business Administration questioned why they wanted to get into the food business since they didn't have previous restaurant experience. Instead they decided to focus just on their passion: beer.

Rivertown is strictly a production brewery. There's no tasting room or gift shop for the public. The brewery doesn't sell directly to the public. Rivertown is located in a small industrial park in Lockland, a suburb just north of Cincinnati. The operation is small, pumping out about fifteen hundred barrels a year.

A majority of their beer is sold in bottles—the smaller heritage bottles like Sierra Nevada as opposed to longnecks. They also keg their beer. They have lofty goals for the brewery.

"We're definitely not going to try to be a Budweiser or Coors or anything like that. Twenty years from now maybe a Sam Adams," Schiltz said.

Roeper serves as the master brewer. And it's easy to see why. He has an impressive homebrewing background.

An entire wall in the small brewery office is devoted to medals, certificates, and blue, red, and yellow ribbons won through the years. There's also a giant poster commemorating Roeper as a finalist in the 2009 Samuel Adams Longshot competition, which honors the best homebrewers in the country. He earned the accolade for an unblended lambic. The poster is signed by Boston Beer Company founder Jim Koch.

Cincinnati can be a tough market for craft brewers, Roeper said. Why? Well, at one time the community was filled with German-inspired regional brewers who made, in Roeper's words, "yellow piss water." And that's what many people in Cincinnati still want, he said.

Early on, Rivertown focused on German-style beers, such as a helles, dunkel, and hefeweizen, to ease into the market, but Rivertown and another local craft brewer, Mt. Carmel Brewing, are helping to expand local tastes.

The flagship beer for Rivertown is Hop Bomber Pale Ale.

"Well-balanced pale ale. Sixty IBU. 5.5 percent alcohol," Schiltz said when asked to describe it. "It is hoppy but has a nice malt backbone, and rye just to give it enough spiciness to go along with the hops."

Beers brewed: Year-round: Helles Lager, Hefeweizen, Dunkle, Oatmeal Stout, Vienna Lager, Hop Bomber Pale Ale, and Hop Baron Double Down IPA. The brewery also does six seasonals.

The Pick: The Hop Bomber Pale Ale is hoppy, with a spicy finish because of the use of rye malt.

Rivertown Brewing Company

Opened: 2009.
Owners: Jason Roeper and Randy Schiltz.
Brewer: Jason Roeper.

System: 10-barrel Premier system.

Production: 1,500 barrels.

Distribution: Ohio, Indiana, and portions of Kentucky.

Hours: The brewery isn't open to the public.

Tours: None.

Take-out beer: Rivertown doesn't sell directly to the public.

Parking: There is plenty of space around the industrial park.

Other area beer sites: See page 114.

Rock Bottom

10 Fountain Square, Cincinnati, OH 45202
513-621-1588 • www.rockbottom.com

Rock Bottom may be part of a national chain, but don't let that fool you into thinking the beer at its brewpubs is mass-produced in some faraway brewery.

Each restaurant has its own brewer with 100 percent freedom to create beer that suits the local market. Walk into the Rock Bottom in Cincinnati or the one in Pittsburgh or Phoenix or Denver and you'll find locally made beer that's unique to those communities.

It's a business philosophy that sets the company apart from other chains that offer the same recipes at each location. Even the craft brewing community has recognized Rock Bottom's contribution to the industry. The Brewers Association, a trade group in Boulder, Colorado, awarded the company its "Large Brewpub and Large Brewpub Brewer of the Year" award in 2008.

The Rock Bottom story dates back to 1976 when founder Frank B. Day opened the first Old Chicago restaurant in Boulder. The restaurant group ultimately expanded into beer and runs more than 140 restaurants, including more than forty brewpubs operating under the names Rock Bottom, ChopHouse, Sing Sing, and the Walnut Brewery. The first Rock Bottom opened in 1991.

The company was purchased in 2010 and now is under the umbrella company CraftWorks Restaurants & Breweries Inc., which also operates the Gordon Biersch chain.

The Cincinnati Rock Bottom opened downtown in 1996. It's been a staple ever since and was the community's only brewpub in 2008, a disheartening thought given the fact that more than 2 million people live in the metropolitan area. The brewpub survived through some lean times after race riots in 2001 scared many people away from venturing into the center city.

Today, though, the downtown has seen an entertainment renaissance. Boutique bars and restaurants have opened all around Rock Bottom, located in the Fountain Square District. On a nice day, it's not unusual to find the plaza in front of the brewpub bustling with people.

Rock Bottom is a typical brewpub. The emphasis is on the restaurant, as opposed to the brewery itself. There is a long bar for people to sit at, but the restaurant is set up more for casual dining.

The brewhouse, however, is front and center. It is in the middle of the restaurant and enclosed in glass for patrons to watch the beer-making process. At the bar, serving vessels are kept behind glass, and the fermenters are located at the back of the restaurant, but they are visible from Sixth Street for anyone passing by.

Brewer Mitchell Dougherty arrived in July 2007 from Phoenix, where he grew up and did a brewing apprenticeship at the Rock Bottom there. The move was quite a transition for him when it came to beer.

"The West Coast is known for hops," Dougherty said. "Coming out here I had to step back and see what the community wanted, and what's cool about Rock Bottom is they allow us to do that."

It took Dougherty a little while to figure out what Cincinnati wanted. He caught on to the Germanic influence, so his beers reflect that. Cincinnati American Light, an easy-drinking blonde lager aged at near freezing for at least a month, is the best-seller and always available.

"Most brewpubs you go to, if they have a light beer that's going to be the most popular," Dougherty said. "We try to give the Germanic heritage here what they want and brew lots of German beers."

The second most popular is Crosley Field Pale Ale, an American pale ale. People are just starting to catch on to hoppy beers and looking to expand their tastes beyond national brands, Dougherty said.

"So many people come in here not even knowing it's a brewpub. Probably a good 20 percent. A lot of people ask if this is fake," he said,

Beers brewed: Year-round: Cincinnati American Light, White Tiger Wheat, Crosley Field Pale Ale, Tall Stacks Ale, Brown Bear Brown, and a rotating dark beer such as a porter or stout. Seasonals: A new specialty beer is available each month.

The Pick: Always go with the medal winner. Rock Bottom Cincinnati won a bronze medal at the World Beer Cup in 2010 for its Rudolf's Bourbon Scotch Ale. It's obviously a seasonal beer, but if it's there, snap it up.

pointing to the brewing equipment. "They ask, 'Do you guys really use that?'"

Dougherty is an accomplished brewer. He won a bronze medal at the 2010 World Beer Cup for his Rudolph's Bourbon Scotch Ale in the Wood and Barrel-Aged Strong Beer category. And his Sarah's Two-Headed Buffalo won a gold at the 2010 Festival of Wood and Barrel Aged Beer in Chicago.

The recognition reinforced his self-confidence, but Dougherty said he refuses to get arrogant about his brewing skills because someone somewhere is always making a better-tasting beer. His philosophy about beer is simple.

"My goal as a brewer is to give the public what they want. Create a product that has layers of flavor. That's my goal in designing beer."

Rock Bottom

Opened: 1996.

Owner: CraftWorks Restaurants & Breweries.

Brewer: Mitchell Dougherty.

System: A 12-barrel JV Northwest system.

Production: 1,500 barrels.

Distribution: On the premises only.

Hours: Daily, 11 A.M. to 11 P.M.

Tours: Available by request.

Take-out: Growlers and kegs.

Food: Traditional American fare. The restaurant offers basic appetizers and entrees from burgers to Ponzu salmon to filet mignon.

Extras: The restaurant offers a mug club.

Parking: On-street, metered parking and nearby parking garages.

Other area beer sites: See page 114.

Wooden Shoe Brewing Company

69 S. Garfield Street, Minster, OH 45865
www.woodenshoebrews.com

Andy Phlipot wanted to get his father a beer-related gift for Christmas, specifically something related to the Star Brewing Company and Wooden Shoe Brewing Company. Star Brewing was founded in 1869 in Minster and grew into a large regional brewery serving Ohio, Indiana, Michigan, Missouri, New York, and West Virginia.

It survived Prohibition by making soft drinks and near beer and was renamed Wooden Shoe in 1940.

Eugene Phlipot is a big collector of Star and Wooden Shoe memorabilia and can remember going to the brewery with his father. He even has the replicated rathskeller bar in his basement, so that made it a little difficult for his son to find some collectible that his father didn't already have.

That's when Andy decided to get his dad the actual brewery trademarks. The Phlipots now own Star Brewing and Wooden Shoe, and that was the impetus for the new Wooden Shoe Brewing Company, run out of a small houselike building in the tiny town of Minster, a farming community with a population of only three thousand people in western Ohio.

"It's something that's unbelievable," Eugene Phlipot said about the return of the Wooden Shoe brand in 2005. "I never thought it'd happen."

The Phlipots and brewer Marc Pelletier are proud of the Wooden Shoe heritage, knowing that nostalgia could help at least get their foot in the door with beer drinkers. They even use some of the old advertising logos and slogans. One features old-fashioned band members playing the trombone, tuba, and marching bass drum with the saying, "In Tune with Good Taste." Another is "A Matter of Preference."

The original Wooden Shoe brewery, which specialized in German lagers, was a community institution. At one point, the brewery also was the town's water supplier and the taxes generated paid

Beers brewed: Year-round beers: Wooden Shoe Lager, Wooden Shoe Bock, Stallostown Wheat, and Wooden Shoe Canoe. The brewery also does seasonal and rotating beers.

The Pick: Wooden Shoe Lager is a light German lager with a slightly sweet and malty character. There's very little hop flavor and the beer qualifies as a refreshing lawnmower beer.

for the operation of the entire community. It also was a huge draw for hobos who discovered that all the beer that splashed onto the floor ran down a drain to a spigot outside where they could fill up a pail or any other container.

Another interesting fact is that Charles Koch, whose son Jim Koch would go on to found the Boston Beer Company and help usher in the craft beer movement, was the last brewmaster at Wooden Shoe when it closed in 1953.

The brewery, which has been demolished, produced up to 150,000 barrels a year in its heyday. The community, now known more for the Dannon Company and Minster Machine Company plants, was defined by Wooden Shoe in those days.

"We are building this business to be as successful, or more successful, than that," said Pelletier, a former homebrewer.

When the Wooden Shoe brand returned, the Phlipots had the beer made on contract at first down in Cincinnati at the former Barrelhouse Brewing and then at Elevator Brewing in Columbus, where it was made and bottled until 2011. They wanted to start small and see how the market reacted before investing in their own brewery.

After five years of slow growth, the Phlipots discovered their beer wasn't just a fad and people really enjoyed it. They opened their own production brewery in Minster in late 2010. The brewery is just around the corner from the main street running through town and is set in a small blue house well off the road. In other words, it can be easy to accidentally drive by if you're not paying attention.

In 2010, the brewery was the only one operating in western Ohio, and it's certainly off the beaten path, located about eleven miles west of Interstate 75, which runs from Dayton to Toledo.

The beer itself isn't the same recipe as the original Wooden Shoe, but it's in the same style.

"We are sticking with the local heritage of the community, which is a German-based community," Pelletier said. "Our beers are continental European German beers. Lagers. Alts. Belgian Ales. It's a pure German-heritage type of operation."

"We don't want to be on the market as the Kmart of beers," he added. "We want to be the BMW."

Wooden Shoe Brewing Company

Opened: 2005.

Owners: Andy and Brianna Phlipot, Eugene and Mary Lou Phlipot, and Marc and Dena Pelletier.

Brewer: Marc Pelletier.

System: 8-barrel Price-Schonstrom system.

Distribution: Statewide, but more readily available in western Ohio.

Hours: Friday, 4 P.M. to 6:30 P.M.; Saturday, 9 A.M. to noon.

Tours: Upon request.

Take-out beer: Growlers, bottles, and kegs.

Parking: On-site.

Other area beer sites: See page 114.

Other "Breweries"

RooBrew Brewery, Granite City Food & Brewery, and BJ's Restaurant & Brew-house don't have their own chapters in this book and that might have a few readers scratching their heads. There's a reason. Really.

This book is about Ohio breweries and that means beer produced within the state. RooBrew is made in Ohio all right, but it's brewed on contract by Thirsty Dog Brewing Company in Akron. Meanwhile, Granite City and BJ's Restaurant don't brew beer in the Buckeye State at all. Instead, their beer is shipped in.

But it seems silly to ignore these operations altogether. RooBrew is a legitimate business venture and Granite City and BJ's Restaurant are pubs, where people can sit down, have a meal, and enjoy a decent beer. So here's a little background about these operations.

- **RooBrew** (411 Wolf Ledges Parkway, Suite 105, Akron, 330-703-3947, www.roobrew.com) is a joint venture by three successful businessmen: Barry Rosenbaum, Gordon Schorr, and John Myers. They provide economic development assistance to the University of Akron and offer help to other entrepreneurs throughout Northeast Ohio.

  All three owners had made beer before and had a passion for it. After offering advice to other entrepreneurs on how to start a business, they decided to start up one of their own and opted for a brewery.

  Now, if you live in Northeast Ohio, you're likely familiar with the University of Akron mascot. It's a kangaroo named Zippy. The Akron area went nuts over Zippy when the kangaroo was named the 2008 Capital One National Mascot of the Year. Rosenbaum, Schorr, and Myers got inspiration from the Zippy hype and named their new venture RooBrew. They even adopted the university's gold and navy colors for their packaging.

  Instead of opening up their own brewery, the owners approached Thirsty Dog co-owner John Najeway to have their beer made at the Thirsty Dog brewery. After several years in development, RooBrew finally hit the market in 2009.

The main beer, Litigation Lager, is a Munich–style helles. The logo pictures a kangaroo holding the scales of justice and a gavel. The other offering is Kickin' Tail Ale, an American-style ale. The label on that beer is of two kangaroos squaring off with boxing gloves on. The beer is available in both bottles and on draft at bars, restaurants, and retail stores throughout the Akron area. RooBrew is also available at the Thirsty Dog tasting room (529 Grant Street, Akron).

- **Granite City Food & Brewery** (2300 Village Drive W., Suite 130, Maumee, 419-878-9050, www.gcfb.net) is a chain restaurant located in the trendy Shops at Fallen Timbers, an outdoor shopping plaza in suburban Toledo. The restaurant is a classier version of an Applebee's or Max & Erma's.

  The first Granite City opened in 1999 in St. Cloud, Minnesota. Today, the Minneapolis-based chain operates twenty-six restaurants in eleven states. The menu can vary by restaurant. The Maumee site features everything from burgers to steaks to salmon.

  As you might expect from a chain restaurant, Granite City isn't going after the craft beer drinker looking for any wild or high-alcohol styles. Instead, you'll find the brewpub mainstays: light, pale ale, wheat, and stout. They also offer a couple of seasonal selections.

  As I mentioned, Granite City doesn't actually brew its beer on the premises in Maumee. Instead, the beer is trucked in. That's not a swipe at the Granite City beer by any means. It's worth a visit. One bit of advice, though. The emphasis is more on dining than beer drinking. The bar is small and can be easily overwhelmed during peak eating times—just picture hordes of suburbanites descending on the place at 6 P.M. on a Friday.

  The restaurant does sell growlers and has a mug club. When joining the mug club, you get a card similar to a credit card instead of an actual mug. The card provides you with discounts on food and allows you to accumulate points toward gifts, such as hats, T-shirts, sweatshirts, and a personalized beer mug.

- **BJ's Restaurant & Brewhouse** (two locations in Ohio: 1414 Polaris Parkway, Columbus, 614-885-1800; and 11700 Princeton Pike, Cincinnati, 513-671-1805; www.bjsbrewhouse.com).

  BJ's started in 1978 in Santa Ana, California, as a deep-dish pizza joint. It wasn't until 1996 when the first BJ's brewery opened. The chain, based in Huntington Beach, California, operates more than one hundred restaurants throughout the country, with nearly half of them in California.

Some beer drinkers may dismiss BJ's as just another corporate chain brewery, but that would be a significant mistake. Through 2010, the chain had earned a total of twenty-seven medals at the Great American Beer Festival, including twelve gold medals. That means they take their beer seriously. The chain even has a whole page on its website devoted to awards that their brewers have garnered over the years.

The restaurants have up to twelve house beers available at any given time, with eight of those being mainstays and the others being rotating or seasonal offerings.

BJ's doesn't brew on the premises in Ohio. Instead, it brings in kegs. The Ohio restaurants are modern-looking, both inside and out, with exposed heating and ventilation on the ceiling and exposed brick.

The emphasis is on the dining experience, but there is a pretty sizeable granite-top bar where people can sit and watch a giant high-definition television. The signature menu item is the deep-dish pizza, but the restaurants offer everything from salads to steak and pasta.

Northwest Ohio

Northwest Ohio has miles and miles of Lake Erie coastline that attract fish-ermen, boaters, and swimmers throughout the summer season. But Lake Erie isn't the only water attraction. The Sandusky region, an area between Cleveland and Toledo with about eighty thousand people, has become a major tourist destination for people who enjoy indoor waterparks.

Entertainment companies Kalahari Resorts, Great Wolf Resorts, and Cedar Fair operate gigantic indoor waterparks in Sandusky. To be honest, they can't even be called just waterparks. They are resorts. Each has a hotel, restaurants, and retail shops. The waterparks themselves are spectacular, with giant slides, rivers for inner tubes, manmade surfing areas, and enormous wave pools.

- **Kalahari Resort** (7000 Kalahari Drive, Sandusky, 877-525-2427, www.kalahariresorts.com) claims its Sandusky park is the largest indoor waterpark in the United States at 173,000 square feet, and that doesn't even include the 77,000-square-foot outdoor water-park. The African-themed resort includes an 884-room hotel, giant convention center, retail shops, spa, miniature golf course, and restaurants. Kalahari also operates a waterpark resort in Wisconsin Dells, Wisconsin, and plans to build one in Fredericks-burg, Virginia.

- **The Great Wolf Lodge** (4600 Milan Road, Sandusky, 419-609-6000, www.greatwolf.com) is another gigantic waterpark at 42,000 square feet. The kid-centric, woodsy-themed park includes a 271-room hotel, meeting space, restaurants, and gift shop. Great Wolf Resorts has twelve indoor waterparks, including another Ohio resort in Mason near Cincinnati.

- **Castaway Bay** (2001 Cleveland Road, Sandusky, 419-627-2106, www.castawaybay.com) is operated by Cedar Fair Entertainment Company, which also owns the Cedar Point amusement park. The tropical-themed resort has 237 hotel rooms and a 38,000-square-foot waterpark. There also are restaurants and retail shops.

- **Cedar Point** (1 Cedar Point Drive, Sandusky, 419-627-2350, www .cedarpoint.com) has been rated the Best Amusement Park in the world for more than a dozen years by *Amusement Today*, a monthly trade newspaper. The park is considered a must-visit for roller coaster fanatics. The park has seventeen roller coasters, including the 310-foot-tall Millennium Force, which has been named Best Steel Roller Coaster in the World and tops out at 93 miles per hour.

  Cedar Point also operates an 18-acre outdoor waterpark called **Soak City.** The park includes more than two dozen water slides, two inner tube rivers, a 500,000-gallon wave pool, and family raft ride. It's open Memorial Day weekend through Labor Day.

Obviously, Northwest Ohio is more than just indoor waterparks and an entertaining amusement park. It's also where you'll find the Lake Erie islands, a popular seasonal attraction and home to—amazingly—four brewpubs. The islands aren't exactly the easiest places to visit and they shut down during the winter. You'll have to hop on either a fast ferry or a slow one.

- **The Jet Express** (3 N. Monroe Street, Port Clinton, 800-245-1538, www.jet-express.com) offers service to Put-in-Bay and Kelleys Island. It's a passenger ferry only and leaves from both Port Clinton and Sandusky.

- **The Miller Boat Line** (535 Bayview Avenue, Put-in-Bay, 800-500-2421, www.millerferry.com) offers service to Put-in-Bay and Middle Bass Island. You can take your car on the ferry.

- **The Kelleys Island Ferry** (510 W. Main Street, Marblehead, 419-798-9763, www.kelleysislandferry.com) takes passengers and vehicles to Kelleys Island. There also is a small boat, the Sonny S. Ferry, that runs a limited schedule from Put-in-Bay to Middle Bass Island.

The area is known for walleye fishing; Port Clinton, a small city on the lake, calls itself the "Walleye Capital of the World." The community has a goofy tradition of dropping a twenty-foot, six-hundred-pound walleye at the stroke of midnight on New Year's Eve instead of a ball like in Times Square in New York.

Toledo, the state's fourth-largest city with more than 300,000 people, also is here. Toledo sits on the border of Michigan and is a spot where the intense Ohio State University and University of Michigan football rivalry can split families and neighbors.

At its heart, Toledo is a working-class city with strong ties to the auto and glass making industries. Detroit is just an hour north so it's no surprise that Chrysler, General Motors, and Dana Holding Corporation employ thousands of workers at automotive and parts plants in the area. Glass manufacturers Owens Corning, Owens-Illinois, and Libbey Inc. are all headquartered in Toledo. Thanks to its rich heritage of glassmaking, the city carries the nickname the Glass City.

- **The Toledo Museum of Art** (2445 Monroe Street, Toledo, 419-255-8000, www.toledomuseum.org) features a special collection of more than five thousand glass pieces ranging from ancient to modern times. The display is housed in the 74,000-square-foot Glass Pavilion.

Outside of Toledo and Sandusky, you'll find the small communities of Bowling Green, Tiffin, Findlay, Lima, and Defiance. The majority of Northwest Ohio is dominated by farmland.

Here are some beer-related options in the area.

- **Granite City Food & Brewery** (2300 Village Drive W, Suite 130, Maumee, 419-878-9050, www.gcfb.net) is part of a corporate chain based in Minneapolis. The restaurant trucks in its namesake beer instead of brewing on premises (see page 142).

- **The Beer and Wine Cave** (4400 Heatherdowns Boulevard, Toledo, 419-382-6221, www.thebeerandwinecave.com) offers an impressive selection of beer and routinely holds beer and wine sampling events.

- **Daddy Oh's Pub & Deli** (4044 Monroe Street, Toledo, 419-473-9100) may look like just another dive bar from the outside, but it offers an impressive selection of more than one hundred craft beers. It has been rated highly by BeerAdvocate.com reviewers.

- **Tony Packo's** (www.tonypackos.com) is a Toledo institution. The restaurant chain, with five locations, has been serving authentic Hungarian food since 1932. Tony Packo's got a huge boost when it was mentioned on the television show *M*A*S*H*. Actor Jamie Farr, a Toledo native, played Corp. Max Klinger in the show. During one episode, Klinger talks fondly about Tony Packo's having the best Hungarian hot dogs. The restaurant also has an impressive set of celebrity autographs on display—but instead of signing a photo or piece of paper, the celebrities have signed hot dog buns, a tradition started by Burt Reynolds in 1972. Those hot dog buns are encased in plastic and hang on the walls at the original restaurant at 1902 Front Street.

Here are some other points of interest in Northwest Ohio.

- **African Safari Wildlife Park** (267 Lightner Road, Port Clinton, 419-732-3606, www.africansafariwildlifepark.com). If animals are your game, this park allows you to drive through a safari featuring more than fifty African species. There also are animal shows.

- **The Frogtown Froggy Museum** (136 Summit Street, Suite 1A, Toledo, 419-944-8806, www.frogtownfroggymuseum.webs.com) is an offbeat place featuring more than 350 frogs and frog-related items on display such as clocks and telephones.

Great Black Swamp Brewing Company

Toledo, OH

3323 Monroe Street, Toledo, OH 43604
419-973-1256 • www.greatblackswampbrewing.com

After living in Oregon state, Paul Traver had a hard time adjusting when he and his wife relocated to Toledo. Not that he didn't enjoy his new city. He just realized that he moved from a craft beer mecca where even the smallest community has a brewpub to an area that's still discovering the craft industry

"It was a huge change," he said. "I was in Eugene and there are about 150,000 people in Eugene, and I think there were five microbreweries in the city. Plus you have Rogue that's just over an hour away in Newport. You've got Portland three hours to the north and there are twenty-something breweries there. So yeah, it was a big change. It was a huge shock."

Toledo has a population of about three hundred thousand, but the only brewery around at that time was Maumee Bay Brewing Company. Traver, a longtime homebrewer, had always want-

Beers brewed: Year-round: Sand Piper Golden Ale, Mosquito Red, Bull Frog Stout, Bay Front Pale Ale, and Wild Duck India Pale Ale. They also make rotating and seasonal beers.

The Pick: Mosquito Red is a light, easy-drinking beer that's heavier on the malt than the hops.

ed to become a professional brewer and saw an opportunity with only one brewery in the community. He hooked up with Bob Morris, who helped start the Salacious Homebrewers In Toledo club in 1989, and they opened Great Black Swamp Brewing in late 2010. (Morris joked that "When you say our beer tastes like shit, that's a compliment.")

Traver was working at a market research company before leaving his job to open the brewery. He also previously had worked at a home-brew shop. Morris works in real estate and rental housing. They share brewing duties.

The brewery name may sound familiar. There was a Black Swamp Brewing in Toledo years ago, and Morris was one of the folks involved in that operation. It didn't last long, though, and Morris said it was more of a hobby than a serious brewery. They figured they would play off that original name and logo. The logo of the old operation was a frog and the new one is a leopard frog, which has spots on its back.

Great Black Swamp is in a tan concrete-block building along a down-trodden section of Monroe Street. It's an area filled with little strip malls and commercial buildings just northwest of the heart of down-town. From the road, the brewery building appears abandoned. There isn't even a sign out front promoting the business. And that's all right with Traver and Morris.

Great Black Swamp is strictly a production brewery making draft beer only, so there isn't much interaction with the public at the site. In the future, Traver and Morris figure they might erect a sign featuring just the leopard frog logo outside and not the name of the brewery. The folks who know about the brewery would recognize the logo and understand what's there, they said.

Traver and Morris cobbled together a mix-and-match brewhouse. The two fermenters are the most interesting pieces of equipment. They are old, half-moon-shaped dairy tanks. Great Black Swamp does con-trolled open fermentation. While the fermenters aren't sealed tight, they do have lids that are kept closed, and there's enough of a carbon diox-ide blanket that forms over the soon-to-be beer to protect the liquid.

Great Black Swamp had been open for only two weeks when I visit-ed in December 2010. The brewery was still getting off the ground, determining where the beer would be available and updating its web-site. Traver and Morris also were exploring whether to sell the beer in growlers—something that wasn't immediately available when they opened.

Still, the brewery had five beers available. Those beers are the typ-ical ones you'd see at any production brewery—a golden ale, red, stout, pale ale, and India pale ale—all with swamp-related names such as Mosquito Red. They also planned to make some rotating and seasonal beers.

"We're trying to get as much market share as possible," Traver said laughing when asked what their goals are for the business. "Because of our distribution brewery, our lineup is pretty standard so that we have the most appeal possible."

Toledo is a blue-collar community made up of a lot of factory workers so Great Black Swamp has to break people from the habit of just ordering whatever is on draft for a buck, Morris said. That attitude is slowly changing as more bars expand their draft lineups, he said.

"We're really trying to, as much as possible, appeal to the trend of people supporting local businesses," Traver said. "It's gotten to be something that's more important to Toledo over the last four or five years."

Great Black Swamp Brewing Company

Opened: 2010.
Owners: Paul Traver and Bob Morris.
Brewers: Paul Traver and Bob Morris.
System: 7-barrel custom-made system.
Production: 350 barrels.
Distribution: Northwest Ohio.
Tours: Upon request.
Take-out beer: Cylinders. The brewery plans to add growlers.
Parking: Small lot behind the building.
Other area beer sites: See page 147.

Hazards Island Microbrewery

1223 Fox Road, Middle Bass Island, OH 43446
800-837-5211 • www.sthazards.com

Hazards Island Microbrewery isn't a typical brewpub. The emphasis isn't on the beer, since there are only two house beers available. The focus is more on the atmosphere that owner Ed Gudenas has created over the years.

Hazards is a little bit of the Caribbean and South Pacific on the Lake Erie islands. The 22-acre St. Hazards Resort includes small, one-story cottages painted in pastel pinks, yellows, and blues. Giant grasses, which resemble bamboo, grow around the bar area. The brewpub itself is filled with authentic Caribbean and Indonesian items.

There's the hand-carved teak bar sitting outside near the pool, teak furniture, a hand-carved six-foot alligator, and real palm trees from Florida.

Beers brewed: St. Hazards Ale and Summer Blonde Ale.

The Pick: The Summer Blonde Ale is a light beer with a punch for a light at 6 percent alcohol.

The interior of the main bar is filled with photos of the Caribbean taken by Gudenas. There are photos of musician Jimmy Buffett, fake parrots sitting on perches, and paintings of Com. Oliver Hazard Perry. Perry, also known as the "Hero of Lake Erie," successfully led the American forces against the British in the Battle of Lake Erie in the War of 1812. The bar is named after him.

In a special tribute, Gudenas even bought the sides of a naval ship emblazoned with the name "Oliver Hazard Perry." The steel frames hang on the side of the bar.

The bar, with its high cone-shaped ceiling, has no air-conditioning or heat—just like it would be in the Caribbean or South Pacific—but there's also something there you'd never find in those locations. Gudenas bought some chairs, doors, and even a gate sign from Cleveland's old, cavernous Municipal Stadium, where the Browns and Indians used to play. Some of the bar chairs are made from seats from the former stadium.

St. Hazards was born in 1998. Gudenas had been developing a resort on South Bass Island when he was approached to buy a former vineyard on Middle Bass. At the time, the Lonz Winery was open on the island and was a major attraction.

He figured the island needed a brewery, as well. Another factor was that liquor licenses weren't available. The only way to bring alcohol to the resort was to obtain a brewing license. So he bought a custom-made two-barrel brewing system.

"Unfortunately the winery closed in the year 2000," Gudenas said. "That really was a major blow to the island. At that point, we had to become the main reason for people to come here."

He traveled to Bali, Indonesia, to purchase authentic South Pacific merchandise and brought over seven ocean containers of items to upgrade the tropical-themed resort.

St. Hazards is by no means easy to get to. There are only two ways onto the island: by boat or by airplane. There's a small airstrip for the wealthy residents who fly their private planes back and forth. Most people come by pleasure boat or by ferry from the mainland. There are only two bars on the island, Hazards and J. F. Walleye's, and they maintain a stiff rivalry for customers.

For years, Hazards produced only one beer, a strong American ale, and Gudenas admitted it was hit or miss in terms of quality. It also was difficult to find someone to brew the beer, since St. Hazards is a seasonal business. When the partygoers who frequent the island start to fall off after Labor Day, the resort shuts down until the spring.

The beer is better now and more consistent thanks to the hiring of Clint McLaughlin, an assistant brewer at Maumee Bay Brewing Company in nearby Toledo. McLaughlin comes to brew when needed. Hazards is by no means a big operation. Gudenas estimated that he produces only six barrels a year.

In 2010, Hazards started making a Summer Blonde Ale. It was a light beer with only 93 calories but 6 percent alcohol. It went over well with the party crowd that visits the island during the summer.

Hazards Island Microbrewery

Opened: 1998.

Owner: Ed Gudenas.

Brewer: Clint McLaughlin.

System: 2-barrel custom-made system.

Production: 6 barrels.

Distribution: At the brewpub only.

Hours: The peak season is Memorial Day to Labor Day, and the bar is generally open Monday through Thursday and Sunday, 10:30 A.M. to 2:30 A.M., and Friday and Saturday, 8:30 A.M. to 2:30 A.M. Call for times outside those dates, because hours are dependent on good weather.

Tours: None.

Take-out beer: Gudenas said he plans to add growlers in 2011 and also do some bottling.

Food: Upscale bar food ranging from seafood to burgers.

Parking: There's parking outside the brewpub, but it's often strange to see cars there since most people taking the ferry across don't bring their vehicles. St. Hazards has a shuttle bus that picks people up from the ferry docks.

Other area beer sites: See page 147.

J. F. Walleye's Microbrewery

FINE FOOD • YOUR FAVORITE DRINKS
GOOD TIMES WITH GREAT FRIENDS

1810 Fox Road, Middle Bass Island, OH 43446
419-285-2739 • www.jfwalleyes.net

J. F. Walleye's Microbrewery just might be one of the most difficult brewpubs to visit in the country. The brewpub is on the sparsely populated Middle Bass Island in Lake Erie. Unless you own an airplane or boat, the only direct way onto the island is a leisurely forty-five-minute ferry ride aboard the Miller Boat Line, which serves both South Bass and Middle Bass.

Only about forty people live on the island year-round. So the brewpub isn't even open all year. It's likely closed from November until April, depending on the weather, of course.

The Lake Erie islands—South Bass, home to Put-in-Bay, and Kelleys Island—are considered seasonal party spots. Not so much with Middle Bass. There are only two bars on the island. Surprisingly both brew beer. The other is St. Hazards, located just down the road.

J. F. Walleye's was founded in 1998 by Bill Gross, a Michigan resident who thought Middle Bass would be a great spot for a bar and restaurant. At the time, the Lonz Winery was open and Gross figured that a brewery would complement the winery. The winery shut down, though, in 2000 and tourism dried up.

J. F. Walleye's had a full brewhouse operation when it first opened, but the brewpub burned to the ground in October 2002 after an accident while deep-frying a turkey. Gross rebuilt the business and reopened in July 2003. Instead of installing a whole new brewhouse, he opted to buy a Brew Magic Brewing System, basically a small brewery on wheels.

Chris Zeitler and Marika Gross took over the operation in 2005, gambling that eventually the tourists would return. They have, thanks to the state of Ohio opening a marina across the road from the brewpub.

Zeitler and Gross built a wading pool, waterfall, and grotto onto the back of the restaurant called Blue Lagoon. It's a nice spot to cool off on a hot summer day.

Beers brewed: Year-round beers: Light and Dark.

The Pick: Brewer Dan Blatt, who started in 2011, was just beginning to experiment with the recipes at the time of this writing. His mocha porter, which was called "Dark," is the perfect choice for anyone who enjoys a coffee flavor in their dark beer.

Zeitler served as the brewer for years and admitted that early on there was really only one reason he had the brewery: to serve liquor. J. F. Walleye's wasn't able to secure a liquor license, so getting a brewing license, although expensive, was the best way to open a bar.

Dan Blatt was hired as the brewer in 2011 and Zeitler is determined to improve the reputation of the beer. J. F. Walleye's even entered the first-ever International Beer Fest in Cleveland with two new beers: a mocha porter and a blackberry Kolsch. Those are far cries from the plain-Jane Light, a pale ale, and Dark, an Irish red, which had been made for years.

"This is a small step in getting the product out there and getting the name out there," Blatt said about entering a professional competition. "Right now, nobody really knows about it at all and we're hoping to change that." He described J. F. Walleye's as a "nanobrewery"—the trendy term for tiny operations.

The Walleye's beer had always been suspect before and for good reason. The water quality on the island stinks for brewing. But Blatt found a solution to that: He brings about one hundred gallons of water over on the ferry when he's ready to make beer. He hopes improving the brewpub's beer will lead to a larger brew system.

During the prime summer season, J. F. Walleye's can be "insane," as Zeitler puts it. The restaurant, which specializes in, what else, Lake Erie-caught perch, can serve five hundred to seven hundred people a day.

J. F. Walleye's Microbrewery

Opened: 1998.

Owners: Chris Zeitler and Marika Gross.

Brewer: Dan Blatt.

System: Brew Magic Brewing System.

Production: Depends on the tourists.

Distribution: On the premises only.

Hours: From Memorial Day to Labor Day, the brewpub is open daily, 8 A.M. to midnight and later on the weekends. Out of season, the hours vary.

Tours: None.

Take-out beer: None.

Food: Basic American cuisine, with everything from appetizers to burgers and pizza. J. F. Walleye's also serves breakfast.

Extras: There's a small gift shop that sells Middle Bass Island and J. F. Walleye's merchandise. The restaurant also sometimes has live bands.

Parking: On-site parking.

Other area beer sites: See page 147.

Kelleys Island Brewery

504 W. Lakeshore Drive,
Kelleys Island, OH 43438
419-746-2314
www.kelleysislandbrewpub.com

Patti Johnson admits to being a beer groupie. Not in some weird way, but she's just really into beer. She's fascinated by brewers who are exceptional at their craft.

She loves tasting different beer and educating others that there's more out there than mass-produced national brands. So it should come as no surprise that, after twelve years as a schoolteacher, she decided to start a brewery of her own. Her father and uncle had built a small ice cream stand on Kelleys Island in 1960. It later morphed into a breakfast and lunch place, and then dinner was added.

Johnson thought it would be the perfect setting for a brewpub. She had seen the success of the nearby Great Lakes Brewing Company in Cleveland and started researching what it would take to start her own operation. She bought a small Century system in 1999 and the Island Café & Brew Pub was born. The name was changed in 2002 to Kelleys Island Brewery.

That also was the time that Johnson met her future husband and brewer, Doug Muranyi.

"We have a romance story behind this brewery," Johnson laughed.

As with the other breweries on the Lake Erie islands, the Kelleys Island Brewery isn't easy to just pop into. It's at least a twenty-minute ferry ride, either on the Kelleys Island Ferry from Marblehead or the Jet Express from Port Clinton and Sandusky. The ferry rides offer incredible vistas of the mainland, the islands, the lake itself, and the Cedar Point Amusement Park, with its giant roller coasters rising up from the ground in the distance.

Kelleys Island isn't big. Although it's the largest American island on Lake Erie, it measures only about four square miles. Like the other nearby islands, Kelleys is considered a summer party spot,

Beers brewed: Angler's Ale, Anniversary Ale, Dawg Bizkit Brown, Island Devil, and Gale Force Ale.

The Pick: The Island Devil is deceiving. It's a double Belgian-style ale. While some Belgians can be intimidating, the flavor is subtle here and more inviting to the average beer drinker. But don't be fooled. It's 8.5 percent alcohol.

where quality takes a backseat to quantity for many partygoers. And, just like the other islands, it's typical to see people cruising around in golf carts instead of cars.

Kelleys Island residents insist that their island is more family-oriented than the South Bass and Middle Bass islands. There certainly are other activities besides drinking. The island is home to the Glacial Grooves State Memorial, a park that features grooves carved into the limestone by glaciers. It also is considered an ideal spot for bird watching.

The brewery is an attraction, as well, since beer drinkers are always willing to travel to sample some suds. Johnson and Muryani take the beer production seriously, knowing that craft beer drinkers demand quality.

"They come in here and they're like, 'I want to taste your Angler's Ale,'" Johnson said about visitors. "They are educated. They know that they like an English bitter and they know what it should taste like. And you have to rise to that."

The brewery itself, located right along Lake Erie, looks more like a café than a bar, with most of the building devoted to dining tables. There is a small bar in one section and an outdoor patio that provides a gorgeous view of Lake Erie. The brewhouse is behind glass behind the bar.

"We have a local mission on Kelleys Island and we have a beer mission," Johnson said. "It's about the beer and the people coming together."

Kelleys Island Brewery is a seasonal business. Come wintertime, the operation shuts down. That poses plenty of challenges for business owners. The brewery can serve twelve kegs in a single weekend during the summer.

"You have to learn to manage your time," Johnson said. "Sometimes, you do 250 people for lunch versus two people for lunch. You have to have a crew that can do both. And your market on Kelleys Island? There's some people who come in here and drink Grey Goose every week. They don't care that we're a brewery. They are going to every single bar from their boat and they're getting wasted and listening to Jimmy Buffett."

Kelleys Island Brewery, though, is a Jimmy Buffett–free zone. During the off-season, Johnson worked as a waitress at another restaurant and she hears Jimmy Buffett from morning to night. So she opts not the play his music at the restaurant.

Kelleys Island Brewery

Opened: 1999.

Owners: Patti Johnson-Muranyi and Doug Muranyi.

Brewer: Doug Muranyi.

System: A 3^{1}/$_{2}$-barrel Century system.

Production: 75 barrels.

Distribution: On the premises only.

Hours: In June, July and August, open daily, 8 A.M. to midnight. Call ahead for hours in April, May, September, October, and November. Closed in December, January, February, and March.

Tours: None.

Take-out beer: Bottles and growlers, but not all the time.

Food: The menu changes slightly each year. Dinners include perch, grilled chicken breast, and veggie burritos.

Extras: The bar will have small bands play during the season. The restaurant also does catering.

Parking: On-site parking.

Other area beer sites: See page 147.

Maumee Bay Brewing Company

27 Broadway, Toledo, OH 43604
419-243-1302
www.oh-maumeebaybrewingco.com

Maumee Bay Brewing is steeped in Toledo history in more ways than one. For starters, the brewpub is located in the historic Oliver House, a massive brick complex a few blocks from the heart of downtown that dates back to 1859. The facility, listed in the National Register of Historic Places, houses the brewpub, an upscale steakhouse, bakery, café, theater, lounge with a piano, another bar with a game room, and even apartments.

Then there's the fact that Maumee Bay revived Buckeye Beer, a well-known Toledo brand that disappeared when the former Buckeye Brewing Company went out of business. Buckeye was the area's oldest and longest-running brewery, operating from 1838 to 1972.

As if that weren't enough for history, the brewpub also is a showcase for the Toledo Brewing Hall of Fame & Museum. The huge display of breweriana, including cans, bottles, tap handles, trays, signs, and labels, begins in the lobby and follows a wide, winding staircase up to the second-floor landing. At the top of the stairs, there are items mounted on the walls and glass cases packed with Toledo beer history. There's even a portrait of Maj. William Oliver, who built the Oliver House, overlooking it all.

The display spills into the brewpub, where there are small framed posters honoring the ten breweries—Eagle, Toledo, Finlay, Huebner, Grasser & Brand, Home, City, Koerber, Lubeck, and Buckeye—that once called Toledo home. The collection is so large that Oliver House general manager Neal Kovacik estimates that only a third of it is on display. The rest is tucked away in back rooms here and there.

"We have stuff stuffed in every nook and cranny," Kovacik said.

The Oliver House was built along the Maumee River as a first-class hotel, offering room amenities that were unheard of at the time, namely running water, gas lights, and individual fireplaces. Oliver commissioned renowned architect Isaiah Rogers to design the structure, which features thirty-foot ceilings in some larger rooms. The hotel, used as an infirmary during the Spanish-American War, fell out of favor as other hotels opened in town and served as a rooming house, manufacturing site, and warehouse through the years.

Thanks to the infirmary connection, the Oliver House is considered haunted, with ghosts often appearing to visitors and workers. One of the most frequent apparitions, a ghost called "The Captain," is a soldier dressed in full uniform. Fortunately, the ghosts are friendly. The Oliver House has been written up in many books about haunted places and even appeared on the television program *Ghost Hunters*.

James and Patricia Appold bought the facility, renovated it, and in 1995 started Maumee Bay Brewing. The Appolds also bought the Buckeye brand back from Miller. A fascinating side note is that Miller Lite owes its existence to Buckeye. The Peter Hand Brewing Company in Chicago, which produced Meister Brau, had acquired Buckeye Brewing

Beers brewed: Year-round: Buckeye Beer, Glass City Pale Ale, Falling Timbers Red, India Pale Ale, Irish Dry Stout, and Amarillo Brillo. The brewpub also offers rotating and seasonal beers.

The Pick: The Amarillo Brillo sounds like a hop bomb at 8.4 percent alcohol and 101 International Bitterness Units, but it's really a well-balanced double IPA. The beer was just going to be a rotating beer, but it proved so popular that Koester added it to the regular lineup.

and made Meister Brau Lite at the Toledo brewery. Miller later bought the recipe and the "Lite" name.

Today, the Oliver House, the oldest working commercial building in Toledo, features Rockwell's Steakhouse, the premier steak restaurant in the Toledo area. The building also is home to Rockwell's Lounge, the Maumee Bay Brewpub, Petite Fours Patisserie, The Café, Mutz bar, and North Coast Theatre.

Maumee Bay is more than just a brewpub, though. It's actually two separate breweries. There's a brewpub and a production brewery. Brewers Jon Koester and Clint McLaughlin make draft beer for the brewpub on a fifteen-barrel copper Bohemian system. And then there's a thirty-barrel Century system that's housed across the brick-lined street in a separate facility, which also includes a bottling line. There, Koester and McLaughlin make Buckeye Beer, which can be best described as an American light lager, and anything else they decide to bottle, including the Blitzen Christmas beer.

At the time of this writing, the owners also had ordered a canning line and planned to have it operating in 2011. It would be the first craft brewer in Ohio to can its beer.

The brewpub offers more than ten drafts, with plenty of hoppy options. When it comes to the beer itself, Koester has a simple brewing philosophy.

"I basically like to brew beers that I want to drink and it seems to be working quite well," he said. "I'm a big hop head so I definitely do add more hops than the previous brewers, but I also try to balance out what I like with what you know is going to sell."

Maumee Bay Brewing Company

Opened: 1995.

Owners: James and Patricia Appold.

Brewer: Jon Koester and Clint McLaughlin.

System: 15-barrel Bohemian Importers system in the brewpub and a 30-barrel Century system in the production facility.

Production: 1,500 barrels.

Distribution: Ohio, Michigan, and Indiana.

Hours: Because there are so many different businesses operating in the Oliver House, the hours vary, but the brewpub is open Monday through Thursday, 3 P.M. to 10 P.M. and Friday and Saturday, 3 P.M. to 11 P.M..

Tours: Upon request.

Take-out beer: Growlers, kegs, and twelve-packs of Buckeye Beer.

Food: Well, there are plenty of choices. Rockwell's is a pricey steakhouse, with choices ranging from steak to seafood. The Café offers soups, salads, and sandwiches. The Petite Fours Patisserie is a bakery that sells all kinds of pastries. The Maumee Bay Brewpub offers typical brewpub fare that includes burgers and other sandwiches. It also features a giant wood-fired oven for pizzas.

Parking: There are a couple of parking lots across the street from the Oliver House.

Other area beer sites: See page 147.

Put-in-Bay Brewing Company

441 Catawba Ave., Put-in-Bay, OH 43456
419-285-4677
www.putinbaybrewery.com

Put-in-Bay is synonymous with the word "party." The small village on South Bass Island is filled with bars, restaurants, and hotels that explode with activity during the peak summer season. It's difficult to even walk down the sidewalk in late afternoon on a weekend because there are so many revelers. If having a good time in a crowded atmosphere isn't your scene, then Put-in-Bay isn't for you—at least on the weekends.

Believe it or not, there are only about 130 people who live in the village—and 450 on the entire island—but tourism folks estimate that about two million visitors hop on ferries or take their own boats to South Bass and Middle Bass islands each year. Instead of bringing a car over, which can be costly, many people opt to rent golf carts. The community often is awash with golf carts whizzing around.

Beers brewed: Summer Brew, Watermelon Wheat, Ole Cotton Top Irish Red, Dead Leaf Lager, Captain Barclay's IPA, South Bass Oatmeal Stout, and Pass Out Bourbon Stout.

It's in this setting where you'll find the Put-in-Bay Brewing Company, which opened in 1996 in a historic two-story former firehouse downtown. Owners Carl and Chris Krueger had worked on the island since 1986, Carl as an airbrush artist at The Shirt Shack and Chris as a waitress at The Crescent Tavern. The couple bought the old firehouse

The Pick: The Watermelon Wheat has a real aroma of watermelon. It has a great watermelon flavor that hits you quickly, dissipates into beer and then provides a pleasant watermelon aftertaste.

in 1994 and made some major renovations to create the island's first and only microbrewery.

The brewpub itself is relatively skinny, with a giant, old-fashioned wooden bar on one side. It has a definitive brewpub feel, with exposed brick on one wall and exposed heating and ventilation overhead.

The small brewhouse is up front behind glass, giving people an opportunity to watch Carl Krueger make the beer. The back of the restaurant opens up to where there's more seating and a two-story ceiling. There are large mirrors on the walls and also a big-screen television. The brewpub also features a dance club and is home for entertainer Ray Fogg, known as the "Island Rock God."

Put-in-Bay is a seasonal destination; that creates a distinct challenge for the brewery, which uses malt extract to brew its beers because of the brewery's size and the resort nature of the brewpub. The peak season is from Memorial Day through Labor Day. The Kruegers try to have four or five house beers available at all times, with the best selling being Summer Brew, a wheat beer with a lemon accent. The brewpub doesn't bottle its beer so it's available only on draft.

"Because of the fact that we are located on what some people would refer to as a 'party island,' we are repeatedly trying to educate the domestic beer drinkers to try something different," Chris Krueger said.

It's not always crazy on the island. There are plenty of things to see and do that have nothing to do with overindulging in food and drink. The island is home to Perry's Victory & International Peace Memorial, a 352-foot column with an observation platform. There's also Perry's Cave, a limestone cave forty feet underground; Crystal Cave, the world's largest geode; Heineman Winery; and the Antique Car Museum.

"If you like to be amongst all the action, then Put-in-Bay weekends are suitable for you," Chris Krueger said. "However if you prefer a quiet, more relaxed atmosphere, we suggest that you visit during the week."

Put-in-Bay Brewing Company

Opened: 1996
Owners: Carl and Chris Krueger
Brewer: Carl Krueger
System: 8.5-barrel Price Schonstrom system
Production: 125 to 170 barrels
Distribution: The beer is available only at the brewpub and only on draft.
Hours: Open from May to October, daily from 11 A.M. to 2:30 A.M.

Tours: None, but workers are happy to explain the brewery process.

Take-out beer: Growlers are available.

Food: The full menu has typical brewpub fare, ranging from burgers to salads to pizza.

Extras: Put-in-Bay Brewing also features a dance club and is home to entertainer Ray Fogg.

Parking: There is on-street parking.

Other area beer sites: See page 147.

Sugar Ridge Brewery

26963 Eckel Road, Suite 203, Perrysburg, OH 43551
419-367-3851

The Sugar Ridge Brewery name carries a subtle message that most people won't pick up on. Many folks from Northwest Ohio will think the business is named after Sugar Ridge, a tiny nearby crossroads and the birthplace of restaurant mogul Bob Evans. But that's not the case.

Owner and brewer Mike Mullins prefers the malt character of a beer to a bitter hop profile. So he thought having the word "sugar" in his brewery's name would be perfect. The fact that Sugar Ridge is nearby is a great bonus. Many well-respected European breweries use sugar to sweeten the flavor of their beer.

"I personally prefer English-style ales, because they don't have a lot of hop bite and you're going to taste the malt backbone," Mullins said. "That's why I used 'Sugar Ridge' even though it's named after a town near Bowling Green. I used Sugar Ridge as something to describe the beer so to speak—a little more of a sugar backbone, a little more of the malt sugars coming through than the hops."

Sugar Ridge is a one-man operation, with Mullins serving as the owner and brewer. He secured his brewing license from the state in late 2010 and planned to start making beer in 2011 in an industrial park building in Perrysburg, a Toledo suburb of

Beers brewed: Year-round: English Pale Ale, Espresso Stout, and Belgian Red.

The Pick: The brewery had yet to have its beer available to the public during my visit but Mullins gave me a sample of his English pale ale. Many breweries focus on the American pale ale, a much hoppier style. It was nice to taste a smooth, malty pale ale.

about eighteen thousand people. During my visit in December 2010, the brewery wasn't yet producing beer for sale and Mullins was tweaking some of his recipes.

Mullins, who has a restaurant background and worked as an executive chef for years, liked the Perrysburg site for a couple of reasons. For starters, the community enjoys craft beer, he said. And secondly, he lives about five minutes from the brewery.

He needs to live close to the brewery. Mullins works full time for his family's ink-manufacturing business. He didn't plan to give up that job and planned to brew at night and on weekends.

Sugar Ridge will be strictly a production brewery making beer on draft and in 22-ounce bottles. Mullins, a former homebrewer, wanted to focus on slow growth through area restaurants, bars, and retail establishments. He planned to start off with three core beers: an English pale ale, espresso stout, and Belgian red.

Even though he has a restaurant background, he said he wasn't interested in starting a brewpub, because of the amount of time he would have needed to invest in the operation. The production brewery will gobble up plenty of time anyway. Opening his own brewery is a lifelong dream, Mullins said.

"It's sort of a creative outlet for me," he said. "I've always wanted to start my own business, as well. I want to do something I love. I can create things that taste just how I want them to taste."

Sugar Ridge Brewery

Opened: Received state license in October 2010 with plans to open in 2011.
Owner: Mike Mullins.
Brewer: Mike Mullins.
System: 25-gallon Beer, Beer and More Beer BrewSculpture system.
Distribution: Northwest Ohio.
Hours: None.
Take-out beer: None.
Tours: Upon request.
Parking: Lot outside the brewery.
Other area beer sites: See page 147.

Beerwebs

The Internet can be a wonderful resource to get information about beer and breweries. But some websites also can be incredibly outdated, flat-out wrong, or so biased in favor of or against a brewery that it's laughable. So be careful when you're surfing for beer details. Here are some helpful websites.

The Akron Beacon-Journal Beer Blog
www.ohio.com/beer
This is a blatant advertisement for my full-time employer, the *Akron Beacon Journal* newspaper. When I decided to write this book, the newspaper agreed to sponsor a web page devoted to Ohio breweries. The site features maps and a short description of the breweries. There also are photos and videos.

Ohio Beer Guide
www.ohiobeerguide.com
Karen Bujak, the so-called Muse of Brews, runs this guide to Ohio breweries. Karen writes for the *Great Lakes Brewing News* and posts her column on the website. She also provides regular blog updates about new breweries, festivals, and other beer news in the state. The website also features handy maps to breweries, good beer bars, retail stores, and homebrew shops.

HopHunter
www.hophunter.com
The Columbus-based website provides a nice look at the beer scene in Ohio and beyond. It also has video interviews with brewers and identifies great bars and beer stores in the state.

Cleveland Hops
www.clevelandhops.com
Beer fan Kyle Roth runs this entertaining site that focuses on the craft beer scene in the Cleveland area. Contributors include Brad Lantz, Ryan McCartney, and Zac Roth.

BeerAdvocate

www.beeradvocate.com

This website is huge. Mainly, it's a place where beer geeks get together and rate beer. Many of those ratings are harsh and some of the reviewers seem to revel in handing out poor critiques. But it does give you a basic understanding of how the beer will taste at any given brewery. The site also provides a rundown of breweries and quality retail stores.

Ratebeer

www.ratebeer.com

Ratebeer.com is another large site that allows beer drinkers to review beers. There also are critiques of beer bars and retail stores.

Beer Festival Calendar

www.beerfestivals.org

Paul Ruschmann and Maryanne Nasiatka, who wrote *Michigan Breweries* for Stackpole's Breweries Series, run this great site. It provides a rundown of beer festivals not only happening in your backyard but around the world. If you're ever looking for a festival to attend, check out this site. Ruschmann also blogs about his beer travels.

Brewers Association

www.brewersassociation.org

www.craftbeer.com

The Brewers Association, based in Boulder, Colorado, runs two wonderful sites filled with information about craft beer. The group calls itself "A Passionate Voice for Craft Brewers." It's one of the best resources for statistics about craft beer.

Beer Institute

www.beerinstitute.org

The Beer Institute is an industry lobbying group in Washington, D.C. Looking for some industry statistics, such as taxes paid in each state or barrels of malted beverages shipped by state? You'll find them in the group's helpful Brewers Almanac.

Glossary

ABV/ABW. Alcohol by volume/alcohol by weight. These are measurements of how much alcohol is in a beer, either by volume or by weight. Most U.S. brewers measure alcohol by volume. Most foreign brewers measure by weight. If you measure by weight, the alcohol percentage will appear higher than if measured by volume, but really it's the same. So no, Canadian beer is not stronger than beer made in the U.S. That's just a misconception.

Adjunct. Anything added to the beer other than barley that helps in the fermentation process. This can include wheat, corn, rice, oats, and sugar. Beer snobs generally look down on breweries that use corn and rice.

Ale. The term used for beer made through warm fermentation and traditionally with a top-fermenting yeast. Ales tend to have more complex flavors and are not as dry as lagers.

American IPA. A highly bitter beer with, in many cases, a higher alcohol content. Ohio examples include Rivertown Hop Baron Double Down IPA and Buckeye Brewing Hippie I.P.A.

American Pale Ale. A beer with a solid hop flavor but still a malt character. Ohio examples include Great Lakes Burning River Pale Ale and Columbus Brewing Pale Ale.

Barley. A grain that is one of the essential ingredients used in brewing beer.

Barleywine. An extremely strong and flavorful dark beer, with the American version being highly hopped for a big bitter flavor and aroma. Ohio examples include Barley's Barley Wine and Elevator Vic's Barleywine No. 4.

Barrel. A full barrel holds 31 gallons of beer, or about 330 12-ounce bottles.

Barrel-aged beer. Beer that is aged in barrels, often bourbon barrels, although brewers are experimenting with other kinds, including wine barrels. Ohio examples include Rock Bottom Rudolph's Bourbon Scotch Ale and Jackie O's Bourbon Barrel Aged Dark Apparition.

Beer. A fermented drink made, in its most basic form, using water, barley, and hops. Beer is the overarching term to describe ales and lagers, which in turn are the overarching terms to describe individual styles such as stouts, ambers, porters, and pilsners.

Beer snob. Someone who generally looks down on large brewers, such as Anheuser-Busch, Miller, and Coors.

BJCP. Beer Judge Certification Program. BJCP was founded in 1985 to promote beer literacy and to recognize beer-tasting skills. Beers are judged based on BJCP style guidelines.

Bock. A strong German lager that traditionally was made for the spring. A dopplebock is even stronger and maltier. An Ohio example is Wooden Shoe Bock.

Bottle-conditioned. A beer that is bottled with live yeast. The beer ages and the taste changes over time. The beer also is left with yeast sediment on the bottom.

Brewhouse. The area and equipment used to make beer. It can include a mash tun, lauter tun, brew kettle, and whirlpool.

Brewpub. A bar or restaurant that makes its own beer on site.

CAMRA. Campaign for Real Ales, a group that promotes real ale, also known as cask-conditioned ale.

Cask-conditioned ale. Also called "real ale." It's unfiltered, unpasteurized beer that undergoes a secondary fermentation with live yeast in a cask. The beer is served at warmer temperatures and has less carbonation thanks to it being hand pumped out of the cask instead of forcing it out of a keg using gas.

Christmas ale. A beer brewed for the Christmas holiday that typically uses spices such as cinnamon and generally is higher in alcohol content. Ohio examples include Great Lakes Christmas Ale, Mt. Carmel Winter Ale, and Thirsty Dog 12 Dogs of Christmas.

Cicerone. Basically the same thing as a sommelier for wine. So what's that mean? It's someone who is an expert in selecting and serving beer. Cicerones have to pass the Cicerone Certification Program.

Craft beer. Honestly, it's a goofy term created by smaller brewers to distinguish themselves from big national brewers. Up until 2011, craft beer was made by independent brewers who made less than two million barrels a year. The Brewers Association in Boulder, Colorado, voted to change the definition to six million barrels. Why? Well the main reason is because Boston Beer is going to surpass two million and still wanted to be called a craft brewer.

Draft. Beer from a keg or cask, as opposed to a bottle or a can.

Dry-hopping. Adding hops just before, during, or after the fermentation process, which increases the hop aroma and flavor but doesn't boost the bitterness.

English pale ale. As opposed to its American cousin, this beer relies more on malt flavor than hops. An Ohio example is Barley's Pale Ale.

Fermentation. The process that involves yeast turning starches into alcohol and carbon dioxide. The funniest explanation I ever heard about the process came from the brewer at F. X. Matt Brewing Company in Utica, New York. He told me that the yeast is chowing down on sugar and burping and farting.

Firkin. Just a fancy term for a quarter barrel. These small containers are most commonly used to hold cask ale. Many brewers will plop the firkin down on the bar and tap it there for all to see.

Great American Beer Festival. An annual beer event held at the Colorado Convention Center in Denver by the Brewers Association. It's the granddaddy of American beer festivals and attended by nearly fifty thousand people a year. The gold, silver, and bronze medals are coveted by brewers and considered a special achievement in the beer industry.

Growler. A half- or one-gallon glass jug that can be filled with beer. It's washable and reusable. Brewpubs generally sell growlers so people can take draft beer home.

Hefeweizen. A German style of wheat beer with a heavy aroma and flavor of banana and cloves. It's often served with a lemon wedge. Examples include Chardon BrewWorks's Donna Do Ya Wanna and Elevator Brewing's Heiferwiezen.

Homebrewer. A person who brews beer at home for personal consumption. Homebrewers use the same process to make beer as professional brewers, just on a much smaller scale and without the professional equipment.

Hops. One of the essential ingredients in beer. Hops come from the cone, or flower, of the hop plant, which is a vine. They provide the bitter aroma and flavor in beer and serve as a natural preservative. Hops come in many varieties.

IBUs. International Bittering Units. This refers to the bitterness of a beer that's obtained from hops. The hoppier the beer, the higher the IBUs.

Imperial. Brewers have decided to slap the word "imperial" in front of any style of beer that's high in alcohol or overly hoppy.

Kellerbier. An unfiltered lager with a strong hop aroma. Because the beer is unfiltered, it's cloudy. An Ohio example is Columbus Summer Teeth.

Lager. Beer fermented at cooler temperatures and generally with bottom-fermenting yeast. Lagers tend to be dry and crisper than ales.

Lauter tun. A large vessel used to separate the liquid wort from the mash.

Light lager. These are lighter beers with almost no malt or hop aroma. Ohio examples include Miller Lite, Miller High Life, Budweiser, Michelob, and Bud Light.

Malt. Barley that has been germinated for the brewing process.

Mash. The cooking process that turns starches into sugars.

Mash tun. A large vessel used to heat the mash in water.

Nanobrewery. A tiny brewery or brewpub.

Pilsner. A beer that has a strawlike color and is clean and crisp without an overwhelming malt or hop flavor. Ohio examples include Cleveland Chophouse Bohemian Pilsner and Maumee Bay's Buckeye Beer.

Pin. A smaller version of a firkin, usually about five gallons.

Porter. A dark-colored beer with heavy malt aroma and flavor, which has a distinctive roasty character. Ohio examples include Thirsty Dog Old Leghumper and Great Lakes Edmund Fitzgerald Porter.

Pumpkin ale. A fall seasonal made with pumpkins. Some brewers use real pumpkin while others just use puree or pumpkin spices. Ohio examples include Hoppin' Frog Frog's Hollow Double Pumpkin Ale and Thirsty Dog Pumpkin Ale.

Reinheitsgebot. This is also referred to as the German Beer Purity Law. In 1516, the Bavarian government, in an effort to protect the public from poorly made beer, decided that beer should be made with barley, hops, and water only. Nothing else. The law, by the way, has long been repealed.

Russian Imperial stout. A dark beer that's heavy on the alcohol and roasted malt character. Ohio examples include Hoppin' Frog B.O.R.I.S. The Crusher Oatmeal Imperial Stout and Weasel Boy Anastasia Russian Imperial Stout.

Saison. Also known as farmhouse ale. These Belgian beers feature complex flavors, with fruit, spice, and earth tones. They traditionally come in 750-milliliter bottles with a cork instead of a crown. An Ohio example is Rockmill Saison.

Schwarzbier. A black beer in terms of color with a light body, dry finish, and a darker roasted-coffee aftertaste. An Ohio example is Gordon Biersch Schwarzbier.

Scottish ale. A beer that is deep amber to dark copper in color with a sweet maltiness. An Ohio example is Barley's MacLenny's Scottish Ale.

Session beer. A beer that's lower in alcohol that someone can have a few of in one sitting without passing out. The session beer seems to be making a comeback among craft brewers. For years, brewers have tried to outhop each other and boost their alcohol to ridiculous levels.

Sour ale. A really sour beer that's becoming more popular in the United States. Examples include Berliner Weisse and New Belgium La Folie.

World Beer Cup. The world's largest commercial beer competition, held every two years. The event is organized by the Brewers Association. The gold, silver, and bronze medals are considered a special achievement in the beer industry.

Wort. This is the sugary liquid that you get when you mix grains and hot water. It's unfermented beer.

Yeast. Microorganisms that eat sugar and turn unfermented wort into beer.

Index

Other Titles in the
BREWERIES SERIES

Indiana Breweries
by John Holl & Nate Schweber
978-0-8117-0661-2

Michigan Breweries
*by Paul Ruschmann &
Maryanne Nasiatka*
978-0-8117-3299-4

New Jersey Breweries
by Lew Bryson & Mark Haynie
978-0-8117-3504-9

New York Breweries
by Lew Bryson, 978-0-8117-2817-1

Pennsylvania Breweries 4th Edition
by Lew Bryson, 978-0-8117-3641-1

WWW.STACKPOLEBOOKS.COM
1-800-732-3669